TURNING THE FEATHER AROUND

D1608890

George Morrison at Red
Rock, his studio/home on
the Grand Portage
Reservation, 1993.
Photo by Marlene Wisuri

TURNING THE FEATHER AROUND

MY LIFE IN ART

GEORGE MORRISON

as told to
MARGOT FORTUNATO GALT

Minnesota Historical Society Press
St. Paul

MIDWEST REFLECTIONS

Memoirs and personal histories of the people of the Upper Midwest

Eggs in the Coffee, Sheep in the Corn: My 17 Years as a Farm Wife *Marjorie Myers Douglas*
Dancing the Cows Home: A Wisconsin Girlhood *Sara De Luca*
Halfway Home: A Granddaughter's Biography *Mary Logue*
From the Hidewood: Memories of a Dakota Neighborhood *Robert Amerson*

Published with support from the Elmer L. and Eleanor J. Andersen Publications Endowment Fund of the Minnesota Historical Society.

Minnesota Historical Society Press
St. Paul 55102

The paper used in this publication meets the minimum requirements of the American National Standard for Information Sciences—Permanence for Printed Library Materials, ANSI Z39.48-1984.

Printed in Singapore
10 9 8 7 6 5 4 3 2 1

International Standard Book Number   0-87351-359-2 (cloth)
                                     0-87351-360-6 (paper)

Library of Congress Cataloging-in-Publication Data

Galt, Margot Fortunato.

    Turning the feather around : my life in art / George Morrison as told to Margot
Fortunato Galt.
        p. cm. — (Midwest reflections)
    Includes bibliographical references.
    ISBN 0-87351-359-2 (cloth : alk. paper). — ISBN 0-87351-360-6 (pbk. : alk. paper)
    1. Morrison, George, 1919- . 2. Artists—Minnesota—Biography. I. Morrison, George,
1919- . II. Title. III. Series.
N6537.M656G35 1998
759.13—dc21
[B]   97-44821
                                                                                 CIP

CONTENTS

Chapter titles come from paintings in the Red Rock Variation *and* Surrealist Landscape *series, part of the larger* Horizon *series that George Morrison began painting at his studio/home on the Grand Portage Reservation in the 1980s.*

INTRODUCTION

Margot Fortunato Galt

Y*ou know, there are things in people's lives that have an interesting bent or touch, that don't fit other people's ideas or expectations. If people expect just a little story about someone's history around art, that's one thing. But if you want to give it flavor, give it a little punch, then you have to manipulate things around. That's how I see it.*—George Morrison

I first met artist George Morrison in the middle 1980s, when he had moved permanently to a studio on the Grand Portage Reservation along the North Shore of Lake Superior. During those years, I wrote about him twice for Minnesota publications. As I talked with Morrison about his work—the huge wood-collage landscapes, the small Horizon paintings, the twelve-foot redwood totems—I realized how vividly his art brought to life his native Minnesota locale. As my eyes, bred to the Atlantic Coast, gradually adjusted to the North Shore, I began to see rock faces and lake expanse through the lens of Morrison's work.

When I stood on the whale-colored rocks of the big lake and looked out over the water, a "George Morrison sky" sometimes unfolded in playful immensity. It was thrilling to rediscover the truth that art—especially the work of a living artist—changes the way we see the world. The work of famous dead artists—Georgia O'Keeffe or John Marin—had done this for me before. But I liked better having it happen with a neighbor still involved in the transformation only a few miles up the shore from my vacation cabin.

In my early view of his work, Morrison's Native American heritage struck me as crucial to his artistic vision. Only someone whose heritage had been continuously steeped in those scenes could paint them so truly. The Horizon paintings did it best, I thought. I loved the way the small paintings caught Superior's unique angle of lake to sky, its enormous tilt of water pouring toward the shore. They shouted the intense, changeable color of this "Northern Riviera."

Their miniature scale made the lake's expanse all the more grand. For all their artful paradox, the little paintings continually turned me to fresh perceptions of the lake's changing moments. Other artists might depict a scene so compellingly as to make it, forever after, their own. But Morrison's work had the opposite effect—it always brought me back to the lake. His open-handed appreciation of the natural world confirmed my assumption that Morrison's art was of an unbroken piece with his Native American heritage and life-long residence on the shore.

Then, friends who knew Morrison better mentioned that he had lived for many years in New York City and later taught in Providence, Rhode Island. When I heard this, I looked at his work and my initial assumptions more critically. Where had that abstraction, that jazzy color come from? Did my cozy equation—Native artist = native shore—still hold? His works did not ring with obvious imagery; they were not realistic renditions of the lake at all. Finally I had to admit that Morrison, with characteristic wry understatement and deep dream knowledge, had turned up the flame of the lake.

There was no question that I liked his abstractions of the native scene. Color leaped off his brush and smacked a kiss as shocking as the cold, cold water. The sky, lake, and shore were just this electric. Later Morrison told me that at Chippewa City, where he had grown up about a mile from Grand Marais, he and his brothers and sisters used to swim in the frigid lake. By this time I was onto him. I knew that it was not just his Native skin, his traditional Ojibway history, that had wrestled the lake's depth and expanse, its cold and changeable weather, into this uncanny vision. Morrison had lived away from

Minnesota for thirty years. He had apprenticed himself to the styles of European and American modernism—Expressionism, abstraction, Surrealism, and the U.S. innovation, Abstract Expressionism. For many years his horizon cut across distant waters. He had packed his kit with visions and artistic gestures from afar.

Then, unlike many expatriate artists, he had come home again.

Often when American artists take off for the big cities, their neighbors assume they'll never be back. Those left behind take good-bye as an aesthetic judgment—only what's exotic, made "abroad," is the sure thing. If the native son (or daughter) makes good, hometown folks may import their work and shower it with praise. Or, just as likely, they'll dismiss it, blaming its offense on foreign influence. Americans are often more comfortable with art they can admire, or despise, from afar and never have to claim up close.

During his years away, Morrison reaped his share of hometown awards. Would his former neighbors ignore him when he returned, assume that his worth was spent because he was back among them? That didn't happen. As Morrison drew Native American forms into his repertoire, he found a regional audience eager to appreciate his new work. He became ensconced as a native son, whose value was precisely that he depicted the local scene.

So closely tied did he become to his locale that many Minnesotans, including me, assumed he had never left. So we played out the either/or thinking of our "hick elitism": Either the local artist left and became a New York modernist, or he stayed around and practiced friendly Regionalism. Such categorizing has been especially hard on Native artists. The American dream—to leave humble beginnings and find success in the big cities—was not supposed to include Indians. If a tribal member did achieve fame in European dress, he had better remain disguised because if he came home, he might find himself too changed to fit in. This paradox, with all its complications of white racism and Native suspicion, has made it hard for many Indians to live at ease in either world.

For years Morrison has confounded such stereotypes and outwitted prejudice. He left home and stayed away, then returned to study what he had not been ready to learn earlier about being Indian. With rare finesse, while contending with illness and alcoholism, he integrated his Indian heritage with European and American modernism. He has become that unusual possibility: expatriate and prodigal son, avant-garde stylist and tribal member.

When Morrison came home to Minnesota in 1970, to teach American Indian studies and studio arts at the University of Minnesota, he joined a revival of interest in Native American culture inspired by the civil rights movement. Before that, champions of Indian art wouldn't show his work—"It wasn't Indian enough," he explained. Morrison's career has lasted long enough to see a change in such attitudes. Recently, he and other European-influenced Indian artists were designated the "Native American Fine Art Movement" by Heard Museum curator Margaret Archuleta and scholar Dr. Rennard Strickland. This label recognizes that Morrison among others did not follow the Indian "arts and crafts" styles that emphasized traditional imagery. Instead, they were influenced, as Archuleta and Strickland put it, by "modern non-Indian painters, who were in turn influenced by the primitive—a classic example of cross-fertilization."

Though proclaimed an elder in Indian arts circles, Morrison still uses the language of modernism to describe his work. When he went to the Minneapolis School of Art in the late 1930s, there were no Indian artists to study; instead he encountered Picasso and Cubism in a show at the Minneapolis Institute of Arts. He appreciates and still employs Cubism's fractured, overlapping planes. He also studied Impressionism and Expressionism, first in Minneapolis, then at the Art Students League of New York. Some of his early landscapes were painted with Impressionist color and fleeting perception. In New York, Expressionism taught him to manipulate color and figure to convey idiosyncratic moods and spiritual states. His images of the war and an unhappy wartime love affair were rendered in brooding shadow-box dramas.

In New York Morrison also moved away from Regionalist landscape painting. He found Surrealism and its psychological aesthetic more congenial. His landscape paintings and drawings from the 1950s provide an intriguing example of how one artist appropriated Expressionist abstraction (not hard-edged or geometric), then began incorporating the quick, automatic gesture and deep-dream images of Surrealism until, by the early 1960s, his canvases crossed over completely into the new style of the Abstract Expressionists, Action Painting.

For most of the 1960s, Morrison used this gestural and improvisational style, making large, boldly colored, quickly painted works that have the verve, immediacy, and enveloping scale of innovators Jackson Pollock, Willem de Kooning, and Franz Kline, who were his friends. The story he tells of his years in New York and Providence is an example of how one artist made use of European modernism, shown in venues like the Museum of Modern Art or Peggy Guggenheim's gallery, Art of This Century, and spread in the teachings and work of European refugees from World War II. Virtually the entire contingent of French Surrealists spent the war years in New York, contributing to the moment in 1947 when, in de Kooning's words, Jackson Pollock "broke the ice" of the new style.

In his account of these years, Morrison pays a debt to the European refugees who were his artistic friends and mentors. But the Greenwich Village artists, like the Beat Generation of writers who all crowded the Cedar Street Tavern or the Five Spot, also improvised their own venues. The artists held exhibitions in lofts and store-front galleries; they drummed up their own publicity and patrons. In these small shows, Morrison's work hung beside the "big boys" of Abstract Expressionism—Kline, de Kooning, and William Baziotes.

At the same time, Morrison also was establishing himself with an uptown gallery, Grand Central Moderns, where his work sold to museums like the Whitney in New York and to collectors like Walter P. Chrysler Jr., who established a museum in Provincetown, Massachusetts, for his collection, which included contemporary art. The artistic avant-garde had shifted from Europe to New York, and George Morrison was in the thick of it.

George Morrison had come a long way from Chippewa City, Minnesota. Born in 1919, he inherited five-eighths Indian blood; the rest was probably Scot from his grandfather Morrison's side. He is enrolled in the Grand Portage (Lake Superior) Band of Chippewa. His Caribou family relatives came from Grand Marais and Nett Lake, and his Mesaba connections from Thunder Bay, Ontario. Such Ojibway ties existed up and down the shore and inland along lakes and rivers long before French and Anglo voyageurs arrived.

By the 1930s the once populous community of Chippewa City had dwindled. The Morrison family experienced the poverty of the era—no cars, few jobs, few store-bought goods. This was compounded by a gradual loss of Indian power. Fifty years before, an Ojibway, John Morrison, had served as county surveyor for fledgling Cook County and regularly supervised the building of roads. As more white families moved into Grand Marais, however, they took over leadership of the area, and the Indians receded into the background. Their Ojibway culture had been diluted by Catholicism, governmental pressure to abandon traditional ways, and intermarriage with whites.

By the time George Morrison was born, a division had occurred between what he calls "village Indians" and "town Indians." The residents of Chippewa City were less affected by white ways than were their cousins living in Grand Marais. The Morrison family still turned to the woods to make a living. All the children in the family spoke Ojibway until they went to school.

Morrison started public school in Grand Marais. Then a few years later he transferred to an Indian school at Hayward, Wisconsin. Tuberculosis was common among the residents of Grand Marais and Chippewa City, and at the Indian school Morrison was diagnosed with tuberculosis of the hip. Luckily, he was sent to Gillette State Hospital for Crippled Children in St. Paul for treatment. The year and a half he spent there, in 1929–1930, was one of the major shifts in his life.

His talent for woodworking and drawing had been evident before, but when he returned to school in Grand Marais, he began to apply himself in earnest. After graduating from high school in 1938, Morrison entered the Minneapolis School of Art, where he studied the realistic portraiture and still-life painting of the nineteenth-century academic tradition. Soon he was introduced to newer, fresher styles coming from Europe, and he discovered in himself the vocation of a Euro-American artist. After graduation in 1943, he fulfilled the dream of many young artists of his generation by heading for New York.

Though he never denied being Indian, Morrison did not promote himself as an Indian artist. The melting-pot ideal of the period, flawed as it was with racism and war panic, emphasized individual genius rather than ethnic or racial inheritance. When Americans as diverse as Morrison and Kazumi Sonoda, a Japanese-American friend, exhibited their works together, few searched their canvases for hints of different backgrounds. The forward-looking era was enjoying its first avant-garde style, which abstracted a new American essence from the separate modes and genres of older worlds.

Yet, though he defined his art in this new abstraction, Morrison could not ignore the effects of racism. He had discovered what it meant along the North Shore. Moving to New York allowed him to escape the most damaging racial stereotypes, but he still sympathized with others who had to contend with the color line. His own New York friends occasionally kidded him about "the Indian thing." He usually was able to laugh and kid them back.

After his second year at the Art Students League, he spent the summer in Provincetown with friends, where he taught art, did carpentry, and painted Expressionist landscapes and still lifes. The fishing villages of Provincetown and Rockport had become summer art and theater colonies, filled with artists and tourists drawn by the beaches and inexpensive accommodations. During the next decade, Morrison made these ocean towns his second home.

In 1952 and 1954 he won two prestigious awards: first a Fulbright Scholarship to France, then a John Hay Whitney Foundation fellowship. Married by now, he spent a year in Paris and Provence, paying homage to European artistic traditions. He and his wife returned to the United States and lived a year in Duluth; shortly after they moved back to New York, the marriage dissolved.

As Morrison continued to explore Abstract Expressionism, his work became better known. In 1960, teaching at the School of the Dayton Art Institute in Ohio, he met Hazel Belvo, a student in his class. They married that year, and their son, Briand Mesaba, was born in 1961. Over the coming years, their family circle would often include Belvo's two sons from her previous marriage.

By 1963 Morrison was teaching full time at the prestigious Rhode Island School of Design. During the seven years they lived in Providence, the two artists and their sons spent summers on the ocean at Provincetown. There Morrison began collecting driftwood and developing the huge wood collages that marked a turning point in his art. Once again, as he had done as a boy, he was working with found wood. He was also again creating landscapes but now incorporating the large scale of Abstract Expressionism. Moreover, the wood of the collages made a direct connection to the natural world, which his paintings could only symbolize.

When he talks about his return to Minnesota, Morrison recognizes it as the completion of a circle. On the faculty of the University of Minnesota, he began learning about the history of Native American art so that he could teach it. This study and new departures in his art fueled his mature style—the wood collages, the Horizon paintings, and the sculptures based on Indian totems. With the growing recognition in art circles that Indian artists can create with brushes dipped in the Euro-American avant-garde, Morrison has found his work shown, bought, and commissioned by museums that had previously rejected him for not being Indian enough.

Amid this success and recognition, he has been near death a dozen times. It is almost a joke among his friends: George has been dying for twenty years. A lifetime of drinking, poor diet, and inadequate health care, which, as he says, have plagued Indians since the arrival of the white man, all came to a personal crisis in the mid-1980s when he was diagnosed with Castleman's disease, a rare condition of the lymph system. His survival against drastic odds has allowed Morrison to bring the Horizon series to its magical expanse, to enjoy a large retrospective show of his work, and to explore new sculpture based on Australian churingas.

When I saw George in 1994 after a lapse of several years, I sensed that it was time to tell his story. During the previous winter I had heard with distress that he was dying. It seemed miraculous that, six months later, he would stand smiling beside me, stooped slightly over his cane, frailer than I had remembered but, like his brilliant paisley shirt, still strutting with artistic elan. It was time. Somebody should tell George's story.

Over the years many reviews and exhibition catalogs, feature articles and interviews, and one book have chronicled George's art and life. I had written about him twice and applauded and argued with other stories and descriptions of his art. Certainly enough material exists to write a standard biography of George.

The summer day when I met him again, I thought, somebody should gather these varied impressions and give a full-scale treatment of George's art. Then I stopped and corrected myself. No, others should stand aside and let George tell his own story. It seemed the right thing to do.

Timing was compelling. George had survived illness and surgery; he was still vigorous, but his bent posture spoke of passing closer to death. He looked ready to talk to an interested outsider. Ambition had softened, and I sensed that he might enjoy the chance to sit back and review his life.

I also wanted to hear the story in George's own words; I didn't want to put yet another art-critical gloss on it. I had done that myself, coining metaphors to describe the wonders of the Horizon paintings, playing around with the unusual elements in his biography. Outsiders also had formed opinions about Morrison's private life. Before they were divorced, he and Hazel were seen by the press as an ideal "art couple," each a distinctive artist, yet sharing a passion for North Shore images. Hazel's huge drawings of the Witch Tree—or, as she and the Grand Portage Indians call it, Spirit Little Cedar Tree—have gained her acclaim and a following. George's work has enjoyed local and national recognition. All this contributed to the romance that the press spun around them. Then they divorced and, though they remained friends, their understanding of their lives together changed.

Now more than ever, it seemed wrong to put any sort of Euro-American overlay on George's story. Hearing about George in his own words struck me as an artistic and cultural imperative. I wanted the printed page to capture the rhythms and wit, the nuances and contradictions of George's particular way of seeing his life and art. Let his silences remain silences, unembroidered with speculation; let his avoidance of the brag yield its own sturdy pride.

I reasoned that telling George's story in his own words might also appeal to a wider audience than simply the art crowd. George's life illuminates the complications of an individual Indian who has taken an unusual journey away and back.

In the summer of 1994 George and I began the audio taping for this book sitting on a small sofa at Red Rock, the studio/home that he and Hazel built in the early 1980s overlooking Lake Superior. The tape recorder sat between us, and we had coffee, brewed strong and aromatic the way he likes it. We tried to start at the beginning with his parents, birth, and childhood in Chippewa City. But questions about the art on the walls and his current life led us to digress. George is not a linear storyteller. He pauses before answering, sometimes does not answer directly, slows until you think he'll stop, then gathers breath for another long comment.

The second time I visited, George said he had an idea for the title: Turning the Feather Around, one of two Indian names given to him late in life. As children, George and his siblings did not receive Indian names; perhaps too many Ojibway traditions had fallen away by then. The name helped shape the book. The feather of his idea fluttered and showed its spine: George had surprised with a little joke. We turned the feather idea around, exploring its meaning for his life.

He had used his other Ojibway name, Standing in the Northern Lights, as a title for his retrospective exhibit in 1990. I liked the feather as the name for this story—for its associations with flight, with resilience and airiness, with dimensions that vary on either side of a spine, like the spaces above and below the horizon line in George's huge wood collages and little Horizon paintings.

As we talked about the New York years of his life, George leafed through a scrapbook, reading newspaper clippings and commenting on catalogs of shows. About halfway through the taping, George and Hazel decided that her voice should enter in dialogue with his to cover the years they lived together. This gave the book a natural break into two sections. Hazel remembered different things than George, and she gave a perspective on George's family life, on their joint relation to his family and to Indian art and culture, that George himself sometimes did not provide. She also became a point of reference from which an outsider might approach George's Indianness.

I often prodded George on topics where I thought he would have a lot to say. Sometimes he did, and sometimes he did not. Racism is a good example. Initially he was reserved, then he moved into discussing it, and finally he did not budge from a few certainties: "I never said I was an Indian artist; I was an artist who happened to be Indian."

George entered the art world before the heightened, multicultural awareness that we like to think exists today; the guiding metaphor of the 1940s and 1950s was the melting pot. Though Indians were still considered a special case, it seems likely that George—far from home among the multitude of ethnics in New York City—was accepted first as an artist and then second, third, or tenth considered an Indian. We must be careful not to read back into the past the categories and proscriptions of the present.

As with all oral histories, the value of George's tale lies as much in his storytelling and interpretations as in the facts he provides. Listening to George reveals a more authentic sense of what it has meant to live his life than someone else's interpretation could provide. But as with all assessments, George's story must be read with some understanding of how memory heightens or obscures the past. What George has left out or skimmed over can be inferred and considered. Dates, ages of people, details of shows are not his strong suit. Where I could not check these with other sources, I have left them out. Otherwise George's first telling stands, unless we corrected it together.

It is also important to recognize that George is telling the story toward the end of his life. The story would have been different told, for example, before he returned to Minnesota in 1970. As George has grown older, his interpretation and memory have necessarily altered the tale. Some elements have, no doubt, remained the same, while others have shifted in emphasis. Likewise,

George and Hazel occasionally remember differently events that they both experienced; occasionally they disagree. Each reader must gather from the composite voices a sense of what could have happened.

This book does not pretend to be the last word on George Morrison's life and art. But it is his word, and its value lies in the way he relates the parts to the whole and the guidance he gives us through eight decades of an unusual journey. A Native American life told with its own wit and rhythms may help to balance what has been told mistakenly by outsiders.

When the taping was nearly done—some thirty interviews later—I turned to the task of shaping the spoken words to the page. One look at normal-size blocks of prose was enough to convince me that they were wrong for the book; they could not capture the sound, sense, or pulse of George's voice and thoughts. Instead we needed a format that would allow quick connections across time and space, that could highlight sudden touches of humor or allusive and metaphoric language. Short sections fit better.

To introduce each chapter, I borrowed titles of Horizon paintings as poetic hints of George's journey. In the first chapter, "Sky Layer: Attentive Waters," George describes the ingredients in his "magic." I use these descriptions as a motif to remind the reader that the story of his impoverished childhood was lightened by all kinds of magic, some he voices and some he only implies. In the middle chapters about New York and Europe, quotations from reviews of his work document his early success. Then from his meeting with Hazel in 1960, her voice joins George's to recount, correct, tug at their differently remembered family life.

Turning the Feather Around is George's way of gauging and appreciating his life, as he sees it now in his late seventies. Someone will no doubt come along and present other facts, sweeping out the spaces that remained hidden as we sat in the glinting light of the lake. But only George can paint his picture in words, offer us humor and humility in the face of the vast lake, or place bits of driftwood just right to reveal the winding current of his many changes.

For the numerous taping sessions to complete this book, George and I met mainly in our own homes or apartments, but we also took advantage of the hospitality of Mae and Leonard Gilbertson, Schroeder, Minnesota. Mae and her family ran Gunderson's Resort for more than fifty years before it was sold. She and Leonard opened her mother's house to let us sit in a regular living room for several taping sessions and added tidbits about their older siblings who were friends of George's in high school. Later, I worked on the project at a Gunderson cottage during several summers. For me, North Shore hospitality begins and ends with Mae and Leonard.

Another one of our haunts was the Grand Marais Art Colony, where George and I have each taught and attended each other's and Hazel Belvo's evening slide shows, talks, and readings. Jay Andersen, executive director of the art colony, has been a good friend to all of us, encouraging us in the project and conducting a long taping session with George. We gratefully acknowledge his contribution.

George's contacts on the North Shore cover a lifetime; most of them are indicated in the book. But he would particularly like to thank Stephan Hoglund and Adel Tiffany.

The help of Hazel Belvo is recorded in her memories that became part of the text. Briand Mesaba Morrison, George and Hazel's son, also joined in occasional conversations and invited us to his home in St. Paul. Both Hazel and Briand took time from their work and families to talk with us about the project, and we both deeply appreciate their support. We also owe Hazel a debt of gratitude for saving clippings, slides, and other memorabilia of her life with George. She has the historian's instinct for saving and recording; we are not the only ones who have benefited from her foresight.

As we worked on the project, we took several trips to view George's work. Louise Lincoln, curator at the Minneapolis Institute of Arts—a longtime friend of George and champion of his work—arranged, during a busy holiday season, for us to look at early works of George's in storage. For her help and that of Evan Maurer, George's friend and director of the Minneapolis Institute of Arts, we offer heartfelt thanks. Likewise, Tom O'Sullivan, art curator at the Minnesota Historical Society, entered enthusiastically into the project and brought out the society's collection of George's work for us to consider.

We are also particularly indebted to the Tweed Museum of Art at the University of Minnesota, Duluth, and to the Minnesota Museum of American Art (formerly the Minnesota Museum of Art), St. Paul, for their interest in collecting and preserving George's work; they have made invaluable contributions to this book. Our thanks go to all the museums and individuals who have loaned George's works to be illustrated here.

Other artists, curators, journalists, and friends who have written about George, curated shows, and commissioned or bought his work also have earned our admiration and appreciation. Some are mentioned in the text or in the bibliography. We would like to thank particularly those who consulted with us about the project: Mary Morrison Dahmen, George's sister; Elizabeth Erickson, artist, critic, and associate professor at the Minneapolis College of Art and Design; Anastasia Faunce, director of public relations, Minneapolis College of Art and Design; Joyce Lyon, artist and associate professor of art, University of Minnesota; Gina Cavallo Collins, senior associate registrar at the Heard Museum; and Shelley McIntire of the Grand Portage band.

Likewise, we appreciate the efforts of librarians to help us find articles about George—notably Kathryn Heuer of the Minneapolis College of Art and Design, and the staff at the St. Paul Public Library. The latter, including my husband, Fran Galt, could not have been more accommodating.

Portions of this book were created at several writing centers: Norcroft near Lutsen, Minnesota, and the Ragdale Foundation in Lake Forest, Illinois. For quiet and protected writing time, I am particularly grateful. I wish to thank the staff and boards of both these organizations for granting me time to bring the project along.

Finally, without a generous research grant from the Minnesota Historical Society through the guidance of Deborah Miller and the support of the oral history branch of the society, under Jim Fogerty's direction; without the interest and support of the Minnesota Historical Society Press Director Jean Brookins, Managing Editor Ann Regan, and Marketing Manager Nordis

Heyerdahl-Fowler; without the meticulous attention to detail of Press Assistant Editor Deborah Swanson as well as the conscientious and sensitive editing of Mary Ann Nord, this book might never have been completed. Their enthusiastic and timely response motivated us toward its conclusion and gave us valuable assistance along the way.

MARGOT FORTUNATO GALT

PROLOGUE

I've had problems with health most of my life. In the late 1980s, Walter Caribou did a healing ceremony for me. I was very ill, living here at Grand Portage facing the lake. He was in this room.

Walter is an elder, a cousin by way of my grandmother, my father's mother, who was a Caribou. He is not a medicine man; he's an elder who believes very strongly in the spiritual side of the Indian psyche.

He sang and chanted and gave me two Indian names—Standing in the Northern Lights, translated from the Chippewa Wah-wah-ta-ga-nah-gah-boo, and Turning the Feather Around, Gwe-ki-ge-nah-gah-boo. That's how it's said in Chippewa.

For a retrospective of my work at the Minnesota Museum of Art in 1990, I used the first name.

The second name—Turning the Feather Around—also has possibilities.

Feathers have connotations around the world, but the people who use feathers the most are indigenous cultures. Many American Indians revere the feather. In Indian dancing, feathers play a part. I also collect different feathers, eagle feathers for example. My totem is the raven.

George with Walter Caribou at Rendezvous Days, Grand Portage, ca. 1978.
Courtesy of George Morrison

Prior to coming here, Walter said he was going to dream and give me an Indian name to do the healing ceremony. But he dreamed two names—one dream, two names. Maybe I was on my way to recovery. Maybe what he did helped to make me well. You never know.

It's a kind of magic, not like a doctor putting a wand over your head and saying, "You are cured." It isn't that at all.

PART ONE

SKY LAYER:
ATTENTIVE WATERS

My jar of magic—what I call magic—is a mixture of ingredients I put together in 1992. They are listed on a rolled-up piece of paper that I keep in a jar—Chimayo earth, jasper, bloodstone, hematite, cedar needles, sassafras root, Navaho tea, Labrador tea, wild peppermint, mullein, western sage, kinnikinnick, Bernard's tobacco, my tobacco, Cretan sage, and Itsy's tobacco. Itsy is my younger sister Barbara. When she was here for Rendezvous Days in 1994 at Grand Portage, she left me some of her tobacco. I added it to my magic.

I might still add to it. Smell it; it smells good.

Chippewa City, where I was born and grew up, was once a thriving village, with natives outnumbering white settlers. Between 100 and 200 people lived all along the shore of Lake Superior east of the town of Grand Marais. My grandfather, James Morrison Sr., was one of the elders and founders of St. Francis Xavier Church, a Catholic church built in 1895 on a rise above the lake. He usually sat in a gray pulpit chair he had built. The chair was always located to the left of the church door where he greeted people and officiated as the bell ringer.

The 100th anniversary of the church (they also call it the Chippewa Church) was celebrated in 1995, about fifteen years after Father Urban began

1919–1929

George's "magic"

Grand Portage
Reservation

Childhood in
Chippewa City

Family life and work

Grade school in
Grand Marais

Transfer to Indian school,
Hayward, Wisconsin

Tuberculosis of the hip

Gillette Hospital,
St. Paul

the July 4th services to raise funds for its upkeep and to preserve its heritage. The building itself is on the National Register of Historic Places.

In 1930 began the gradual decline of the village. Young people moved away, and old people died. There were few families left. But I remember many families: the Weeshkobs and Filisons, Newtons, LaPlantes, Drouillards,

St. Francis Xavier Church, Chippewa City, 1981.
Minnesota Historical Society

McDonoughs, Caribous, Thibaults, Zimmermans and Howenstines toward town, Beargreases, Rosseaus, Deschampes. I have many recollections of a happy childhood with families and neighbors.

When I stand on Chippewa Beach and look up to see the church, it is the only remnant of my grandfather. The church remains a symbol of the community and our life there.

There are seven Chippewa reservations in Minnesota—Grand Portage, Bois Forte, Fond du Lac, Mille Lacs, Leech Lake, White Earth, and Red Lake. Walter Caribou and my grandmother's Caribou family are from Grand Marais and Nett Lake. Mary Caribou, my grandmother on my father's side, passed away when I was five. I vaguely remember her.

I remember my grandfather Morrison better; he passed away a few years later. Though his name was Morrison, he wasn't entirely Scot, which is where the name comes from. He was part Indian himself; then he married into the Indian nation by marrying a Caribou.

The French and British were the prime movers of the fur trade around Grand Portage back in the 1720s. I think the name Morrison came along with them.

My great-grandfather was born in Grand Portage in 1804, and my grandfather in 1847. They both married into the Indian nations and came about being Indian.

My degree of blood is five-eighths, which is more than half. How they determined that, I don't know. The Indian Bureau has records of that kind of thing to determine your rights as an Indian—what you get from the government in terms of money or land.

When my wife, Hazel, and I came back to Minnesota in 1970—we are divorced now, but still good friends—I became more active in Indian doings and came more often to Grand Portage. We looked around here for a place to live; the idea was to retire up here. We looked all around on the reservation shores, found this place, and called it Red Rock because of the kind of rock, jasper, that's around here. It's part of my magic.

George's mother, Barbara
Mesaba Morrison, and Jack at
Chippewa City, ca. 1940.
Courtesy of George Morrison

My mother's foster mother, advancing in age when I knew her, always had a lot of medicines around in little bundles or little packages, a lot of roots and plants. How she used them or what for, I don't know. Maybe they were medicine, taken internally. Maybe they were used as a spiritual thing, like a fetish, to do spiritual harm or good.

My mother was born at Fort William, as they called it in those days; Thunder Bay today. She was adopted by her foster mother and they moved to the Gunflint area near their relations. Her family name was Mesaba. She had a Sagittarian sign; November 30 was her birthday.

When she was seventeen or eighteen, she got married and started having kids, twelve in all, nine that survived. Her life centered around her children, born one after the other. She had all she could do to take care of us. I was always amazed that she did it in such circumstances, being poor at times, in crowded quarters.

She was very sweet and loving and kind, more loving right along the line than my father. Why, I don't know. Maybe it was shyness. He liked children only as infants; when they grew up, he became more distant.

She was a strong mother. She learned the hard way about cooking or household work, about marriage and the customs of marriage. Starting out simple, she learned by hit and miss, cooking the basics like rice and potatoes and macaroni. She got fish from a commercial fisherman in Chippewa City named Drouillard, who smoked and salted fish. When his nets came in, she went down and got a dozen herring. That became part of our diet. Anything special was store-bought. We always thought store-bought bread was a big deal.

Along the way my mother also started making quick bread. We called it by the Scot word bannock. As the family grew, she made more and more bread. There are different ways to make it. Salt, flour, baking powder; sometimes she'd put in oil like bacon grease. Mix these ingredients up with water; we rarely used milk. Stir it up into a dough, then knead it and put it in a pan to rise. She baked it in our wood-burning stove; it was good when it was warm, especially with butter, if there was butter to be had.

When she made bread with yeast, she'd use a big pan to make many loaves. She also cut off sections and fried them while the rest baked. I hope she was using good flour. I don't think it was white flour. I don't remember. I got into nutrition later. We all survived, so I guess it was OK.

Her herbs and medicine? Pretty much salt and pepper.

Indians in this area lived anywhere they wanted, though there was the reservation at Grand Portage. They lived all along this shore. My grandfather Morrison chose to live in the little Indian village that he helped to found one mile northeast of Grand Marais. Because of the French fur trade, a lot of Indians around here became Catholic. My grandfather held church services at his home right on the lake; then in 1895 he and the village of Chippewa City built the church.

The cemetery where many are buried is north of the church, north of the highway, away from the lake. It is still there. A lot of graves are lost now. At first, only Indians living in the village were buried there, but then later on, with intermarriages, others were buried there, too. They made a new section over on the lake side of the road. The other part is designated the old graveyard.

There's a photo taken in front of the church towards the end of World War I. My father is there, and my grandfather. His wife, Mary Caribou, is in the picture, too; she was a full-blooded Chippewa—a sister, I believe, of Swamper Caribou who lived in Grand Marais. My brother Bernard as a baby is in the picture, and my aunt Julia, my father's sister.

My mother was not in the picture because she was probably at home bearing another child, maybe me.

By then, people in Chippewa City had become separated from the reservation around Grand Portage. Chippewa City wasn't on the reservation proper, and maybe the Indians in town had to pay taxes. I don't know.

My readings and studies of the Indian say that reservations were founded primarily as war measures, to keep Indians in tow, so they wouldn't make any trouble. They didn't get the best land, but sometimes they hit it pretty lucky, like some of the Indians pushed into Oklahoma who found out they were living on oil land.

My people were not forced to relocate. They stayed where they were in Chippewa City. The old road went through there. A small road near the lake. A narrow, narrow road. Then in the late 1920s, they built the new highway. That went through the village, not cutting straight through but along the edge away from the lake.

I was born at home in 1919, the third of my parents' twelve children. Most of the older kids in the family were born at home with a midwife, rather than in Cloquet, which had the nearest Indian hospital.

My father and mother lived upstairs in my grandfather's house on the lake. It was a common structure, probably a log cabin in the beginning. Then along the way, they decided to make it more modern. I remember it had siding when I grew up.

In front of St. Francis Xavier Church, ca. 1918: Grandmother Mary Caribou Morrison, holding George's brother Bernard (front row, third from left); father Jim Morrison (middle row, third from left); and grandfather James Morrison Sr. (back row, left).
Courtesy of George Morrison

When the family grew older, my parents moved out of my grandfather's house, and my father built his house away from the lake on land that is now north of the highway. A small house that we crowded into until the kids grew up and moved away. The house doesn't exist anymore. It's gone.

Some other people lived above the road with us, but very few. Most of them lived below the road, hugging the shore between Croftville and Monker's Point.

The most common medicine we had around the house was wild peppermint. Now it is in what I call my mixture. Wild peppermint was an all-around tonic or brew made into tea, for headaches or whatever. It was very common where I grew up.

Part of coming back to Grand Portage was wanting to come back to herbs as more of a spiritual force rather than just for using in brews.

Years later I picked some mint in Grand Portage. Some people showed me where it was. When I went back a year after, I couldn't find it. Maybe it grows somewhere one time and then it moves.

George's parents and younger siblings in front of their home in Chippewa City, ca. 1940.

Courtesy of George Morrison

My mother did a lot of baking in those old wood stoves. I suppose she just played it by ear, timing the bread. It always came out. The kitchen was the warmest room in the house, with the big wood-burning cook stove. The stove had a shelf at the back that you could slide open; you put food there to keep it warm. Down below were four burners. The one above the fire was the warmest. Way to the right was the reservoir for heating water.

The common wood was birch. We cut it so fast, we didn't have time to cure it. But once a fire was started, you could use raw, wet birch. We used drier wood like cedar or maybe some older birch to get the fire started.

The living room adjacent to the kitchen also had a potbellied stove that took big chunks of birch. That heated the living room and a bedroom. The back room on the other side of the kitchen got heat from the kitchen.

My mother became more Catholic by virtue of being one of many Indians indoctrinated into the Catholic religion by the priests. My father wasn't a churchgoer in the strict sense, but he was religious in that he sang at wakes for the dead. Since there were often no priests around, he read from a prayer book in Chippewa and officiated at burials.

He knew how to understand the hymns from French hymnbooks. Some were translated into the Ojibway language, the Chippewa language. He did have a good voice, and he sometimes sang those songs for practice.

He took the part of leader in the prayer at a ceremony for the dead. The prayers were written phonetically in the English alphabet, but the words were Ojibway.

At wakes he was also a principal singer. That was one of the customs of the day, when they stayed up all night singing for the dead, to keep the spirits alive. The coffin was set in a house, then moved to the church on sawhorses at the time of burial. For a wake the singers, men and women, all sat around the coffin. They took turns taking a break. Then around midnight they had a feast not only to feed the singers but also to make some offerings for the dead.

As kids growing up, we always went to the wakes just to cash in on the feast. We did that for fun. We didn't sing. I guess we probably didn't care about that kind of thing. We had a certain reverence for the dead, of course, if they were relatives, but we didn't do much; we were just around.

Labrador tea is very common. It grows all along my road to the house. The Indians called it swamp tea. It is very potent, pungent. Not many people pick it and dry it anymore. When I do, I put it in a jar and mix it with other teas to make a nice aromatic brew.

I also have some tea from a Navaho person who said, "Take some of this for whatever ails you."

I've put them both in my mixture.

I grew up Catholic but, like a lot of Indians, I wasn't a strict Catholic. There's a little joke about the French missionary having a Bible in one hand and a gun in the other. We were all brought up Catholic, but a lot of Indians, myself included, did it almost tongue in cheek. We had certain Indian beliefs that were inherent. There was bound to be conflict.

When I was young, there wasn't much more than a smattering of Indian stories left. It's too bad when that kind of thing happens. You live in a house and try to maintain certain standards of so-called white living.

The only old Indian thing we still had was a powder horn. That was eventually lost, sold to some trader who was buying Indian curios. At that time the older Indian ladies did quill work and some beadwork, worked with birch bark and even made moccasins out of tanned leather to make some money. But they were gradually losing all of that, even the art of tanning a hide, which was very complicated.

Though some in my village were more resourceful and saved their money, part of the poverty, the violence, and alcoholism revolved around the intermingling of cultures. The Indians could no longer live in their own way— nomadic, killing animals, using the hides for clothing. That was all dying off.

I believe in going back to the magic of the earth and the lake, the sky and the universe. That kind of magic. I believe in that kind of religion. A religion of the rocks, the lake, the water, the sky. Yes, that's what I believe in.

Our play was pretty normal for kids growing up, playing with neighbors who lived in houses all along the shore. We played on the rocks by the lake. When the lake froze over, we used to play on the ice—that doesn't happen very often. We even swam in the lake, even though it was cold. I guess we were tough enough to withstand that cold.

My grandfather had a boat and nets and he fished, but my father didn't fish. My father was a woods person; he made his best living by being a trapper and a guide and selling furs. Beaver was primarily the hide sold around the turn of the century.

They had to stretch the beaver skins. Taking thin alder trees, they made a round frame, bending the wood and tying it together. Then they stretched the hides over it. They had to scrape the inner side to clean it up, scrape off any of the residue from the animal to get down to the hide. Then they dried it. When it was dry, it was bendable, though stiffer than paper.

Lake Superior shoreline near Grand Marais, ca. 1940.
Minnesota Historical Society
(Kenneth Wright)

Then the Depression came and my father worked on WPA projects. Jim, my father, and Joe, his brother, were the survivors of their big family; they were laborers. They helped build the sewer system in Grand Marais. We survived the Depression by getting a government check from one of the Roosevelt programs.

It was a good thing he had this job, but there were lean times anyway. Never anything like starvation, but not always enough food or the right food. Sometimes my father would go out and shoot a deer. Sometimes he went out and didn't get anything. We were brought up poor, but we always survived okay.

When we started school, the school bus picked us up right near our home and transported us one mile to school. I think the bus went as far as Hovland on this side of Grand Marais and picked up all the kids from Colville and Croftville. Then, on the other side, it went way to Tofte and Schroeder. But that was for high school. Tofte and Schroeder had their own grade school.

We could have walked to school if we had to, but the bus was available and it was heated. Later, as people started building along the Gunflint Trail, a lot of those kids came into Grand Marais by bus to go to school. They came from north, south, east, and west.

We talked Indian at home until we were six years old. My father talked Indian and my mother talked Indian and all the little kids talked Indian, until the time we went to school. That's when we began to lose it. We, as children, began to talk English and became so-called Americanized.

You don't take that change seriously until you think about it later.

Mullein is my plant. I got to know it by knowing where to find it. I picked it and let it dry, put it in jars. I put it in tea to give it more potency. It isn't all that fragrant, but I take it because it is related to me in one way or another.

George's father, Jim, and uncle Joe Morrison with beavers they trapped.

Courtesy of George Morrison

We Indian kids played mostly with each other, not with the white community because they lived in town. We lived apart, in the village, the Indians' community. Some of the Indians who lived closer to town were becoming integrated by marriage and relationships with people who were non-Indian or part Indian. We called them "town Indians," but they were still Indians, nevertheless.

I could feel prejudice. A lot of people were down on Indians because, I suppose, the Indians were poor and more shabbily dressed, and many of them were uneducated. A lot of us, of course, were darker in skin. I believe in the color line. This is a racist country. People in this country are predominately white and they are prejudiced against anyone who is dark-skinned. I believe in the color line wherever there is a community of blacks or Indians or maybe Chinese.

My parents would actually say, "We want you to behave and be like a white person." Maybe they meant they wanted us to be educated. Maybe they wanted us to be clean. Maybe they wanted us to behave properly. In other words, not to be too Indian. But how can one change his color? I don't think they meant it that harshly. I don't think they were ashamed of being Indian, but they always looked up to the white man.

My family knew their situation. The only connections they had with white people—not many but a few—were with school officials or welfare officials, the doctor who was white, and administrators who came to our house. My family accepted white people as white people, but they were more open towards their own kind.

As I grew up, some of my family were beginning to integrate a little more through interracial marriages, moving to Duluth and then back to the reservation and so on. But when we played as young kids, we played among ourselves in that little village and not with the town kids because . . . well, they lived there and we lived here.

I was kind of a loner from the beginning because I liked to be by myself, carve, draw, and copy things out of books. Maybe psychologically, I became even more of a loner as a result. They say about artists that they become lost within themselves, in their own kind of expression.

My grandmother and my mother used to carry tobacco that came in little pouches. They used to add it to the fire in the cook stove. Burning tobacco and making the smoke rise up was supposedly to carry the smoke to the spirits. Maybe the old Indians used to throw tobacco in their campfire for the smell and for the ritual, for the magic. That was kind of nice, I thought.

I grew up with pipe tobaccos called Velvet and Union Leader. Both have a nice smell. Indian people used them for their pipes. My mother smoked, too, for a while. Even after she had children, she smoked Old Gold cigarettes. And my father smoked now and then, particularly when he was drinking. But he wasn't a heavy smoker. My uncle chewed snuff.

When I grew up, I used to take some of that pipe tobacco and roll cigarettes.

Years later when my older brother, Bernard, died, all I got from his possessions were a can of tobacco and a heavy, red plaid shirt, one of those lumberjack shirts.

Though there was a little less than a year between Bernard and Mary, and between Mary and me, I didn't know Bernard very well after we were young children. Bernard left home early and went on his own. He didn't finish high school. I guess he wanted to be grown up.

As soon as he was able to work, he got a job, worked to buy a car, and left. I didn't have much connection to him, only the fact that he was my brother. Then when I came back from the East Coast, I knew him towards the end of his life. He passed away early. He was sixty-three when he died.

I regard his tobacco as very special and I still have his shirt, which I wear now and then when the occasion demands. It's a warm, heavy shirt. I also have my own tobacco, Union Leader, on hand all the time. I have some in a drawer over there.

My father's trapping cabin was off the Gunflint Trail on the south Brule River. It sat in a little village unto itself. When we were growing up, we spent weeks there at a time. A sister was born there. It was like roughing it because the houses where we grew up in Chippewa City were pretty normal, with wooden floors. Our cabin had a floor, too, but I'm not sure about windowpanes. It was cold. When you sat in front of the fire, your front was hot but your back was cold.

A lot of the immediate family of my grandfather—his daughters and their husbands, his sons and their families—comprised this little settlement up there, maybe half a dozen houses. My uncle Joe and his family and my aunt who married a man named Joe Thomas were in other cabins apart from ours.

For my father, trapping was more or less big time. He made a lot of money from furs. Afterward, when that ended, cutting wood brought in a few bucks.

We cut a lot of wood for our own use and also to sell. Cutting down birch trees, you have to make trails in deep snow with snowshoes, handmade snowshoes, rounder than most. We would push the snow down around the birch tree, trim the tree and start cutting it down. We used to cut wood in the hills above the house and sleigh it down. The sleighs were homemade, five feet long and maybe two feet wide, with homemade wooden runners.

Trapping cabins used by
the Morrisons.
Courtesy of George Morrison

Then we hauled it to where we were going to saw it. Finally we sledded the wood down to the road so a truck could pick it up. Or we made a cord pile out of it and sold it. We got four dollars for a short cord. Sometimes it would take us a whole day to cut a short cord of wood. But that was good money for those days.

My father died young by today's standards—he was fifty-nine. His brother Joe died at age sixty-four. There had been some smallpox in the family. That was gone, but TB was still a problem in Chippewa City. My father and his brother were the only two that survived from their big family—about fourteen kids.

For many years, the life expectancy of the Indian was about forty years old. Now it's way up in the sixties, seventies, up to the standards of white men, which is in the seventies. For many years, Indians lived hard.

Kinnikinnick is one of the original Indian tobaccos from around this area. It's made from the inner bark of a red willow that's very common along the North Shore. You shave off the outer bark. The inner bark is yellowish white. You shave that off and let it dry. Then you parch it in a large frying pan and crumble it in your hands. It has a nice aroma to it.

It was part of my thing, coming back here and remembering that I'd grown up with all these ingredients. Kinnikinnick became part of my magic.

Of course, Indians in the South grew what we now know as tobacco—tobacco that contains nicotine, which is addictive. It's one of the things they gave the whites. Kinnikinnick does not have anything like that, as far as I know. Indian people this far north did not get southern tobacco until the whites brought it to them.

When I was growing up, I used butcher knives and other knives at hand to carve things out of wood. The idea of picking out a nice piece of wood, I thought was special. I looked in the woods a little but mostly I used castoff boxes or whatever I could find in the neighborhood. I liked being able to find a piece of wood that I could cut down and make something from.

We always used to make our toys from junk piles. We collected an old cart and made a kind of wagon. We took castaway things, straightened them out and made a sled. We were never able to buy a new sled. We fashioned things, instead of being able to afford brand new ones like a well-off family.

We didn't know we were poor. I guess we felt all right among ourselves—kids growing up and playing. We hardly ever played with white kids. We played by ourselves.

A lot of Indians have both cultures. They go back and forth. Walter Caribou, I'm sure, grew up more Indian than English, with more of the old Indian ways. But he certainly lives in a regular house and eats regular meals. Indians are changing with the times. They can no longer live the way they did, nomadic with makeshift dwellings.

White people say the Indian dwellings were very simple. Yet I've heard from architects that a tepee is a very innovative way of putting up a house, a house that can be taken apart and put together again very easily. The Chippewa wigwam is also complex, in the kind of poles and wood that are selected, how they are put together, and even the hides and birch bark stretched over the top, with an opening for the smoke to go through.

The Indians of the Western plains, of course, didn't have much birch bark, so they used hides for tepees. The wigwams of the Eastern Woodlands tribes were rounder and covered in birch bark. They used hides, too, but more birch bark. There was a lot of birch bark available in the woodlands.

I have some sage from Crete in my mixture. It came from a friend. I also include yellow and white sage from the Southwest. Down there, sage is regarded as tobacco is around here. The Hopi and Navaho and Apache burn it and use it in their own rituals, probably in a stronger sense than we do up here. They're retaining a lot of their old customs there, the Navahos especially.

My father and our family never did have many Indian customs. We all grew up in a so-called conventional way.

Sometimes I burn western sage at a meal or function, just for fun, playing the ritual. Here again, it's my own playing around with the magic. I'm not sure why I do it. I think, maybe, there is some kind of a good connection in burning tobacco.

I did play around with a pipe when I went to art school. You know how kids are when they want to grow up and be a smart-ass.

Right from the beginning, my skill in drawing began to show. I used to copy things from illustrations or books. I found myself naturally inclined to draw. Doodling is another word for it, making some kind of images on paper.

When I started going to school, I got things from other kids by swaps. I used to make illustrations for some of the town kids, for their schoolwork. Then they would give me a swap—a jackknife or something.

We got hand-me-downs from different people. My father was guiding for people who came from all over. Some from the South, some from Iowa, and from elsewhere in Minnesota. They came in hunting season. They probably knew that his family was poor and needed hand-me-downs, so they always sent up their old clothes. We always thought it was a big deal. We would rummage through these great big boxes of clothes. We would pick out things we needed.

The Hayward, Wisconsin, Indian school helped people with big families. It was available to a lot of poorer families during the Depression. Things got hard for us, especially during the Depression. I remember eating plain rice, or rice and potatoes together. Sometimes those old staples were the only things around. Now, my brother Mike and I kid about pork grease and potatoes.

As I remember, I was nine when I started at Indian school. My older brother, Bernard, was already there. And Mike started a year or so after I left.

There were maybe fifty to seventy-five boys and the same number of girls, on opposite sides of the campus. There was a central dining room; the meals were adequate. It gave us a good place to eat.

Mary, my older sister, stayed at home. I don't think my parents wanted her to go to Indian school. She stayed home to help my mother raise the children and keep house.

When September came, the school provided transportation, either with a government car or by paying the bus fare for a group of young children. We stayed at the school during the whole nine-month period, and we never did see our parents.

That's an awfully long time. I guess my parents were too poor to come—they didn't have a car and they couldn't pay to travel by bus. They never came to see us. As I recall, we accepted it, we kept busy with the activities, school, and playing. We were in it, so we weren't lonesome.

Many of the kids probably spoke Indian. The school didn't repress it or stop it the way I've heard was done in some schools. It was not a Catholic school, although those who were Catholic went to mass when there was one. The teachers were primarily white. They taught in English.

A counselor in charge of the boys' dormitory was Indian. He was strict but he was not mean.

I've heard stories of the teachers in certain schools being very cruel to Indians. But as I recall, the teachers at Hayward were fairly decent. They all got along with the students and were liked by the students, too. It was all right.

The teachers recognized talent. I was always chosen to do posters and things like that.

During my second year at the Indian school, my leg problems started.

There's a lot of suspicion among Indians, in a sense that they believed in spirits. I guess it's handed down. My suspicion is that my troubles began with an older Indian woman who lived in the village where we grew up. A mean old lady . . . I probably teased her, and maybe. . . . Sometimes you can attribute things to someone putting a bad spell on you. That was just a suspicion of mine.

At the worst point, I couldn't walk. That's when they sent me to the Indian sanatorium at Onigum, Minnesota. But that wasn't the right place for me, so they transferred me to Gillette Hospital in St. Paul, which dealt with orthopedics.

Tuberculosis with arthritis of the hip. Probably tuberculosis, it says in the diagnosis.

TB was common with Indians at that time. My older brother and older sister and my younger brother Mike spent some time in a sanatorium called Ah-Gwah-Ching for tuberculosis of the lungs. They never were very sick from it. I guess the doctors caught it in the early stages and were able to cure it.

At Gillette I was in bed for six months before the operation and eight months after, with both my legs in a cast. Actually, it was kind of a good

Gillette State Hospital for Crippled Children, St. Paul, 1936.
Minnesota State Archives (Wright)

period. I was eleven, doing a lot of reading, and then there was a lot of interaction with the other kids, mostly non-Indian. A lot of others were even worse than I, strictly bedridden. Kids with spinal problems were in bed all the time.

I was able to exchange ideas with other children. The hospital had a good program. I went to school there, was active with art projects, did a lot of reading and became more introspective. There was also a lot of entertainment for the kids, even the ones that were bedridden. Nurses wheeled the beds into the auditorium where we saw circus performers, movie stars, even the prize-fighter Jack Dempsey.

After the operation I was able to walk for the first time in almost a year, but I had a stiffer leg. The doctors had fused the hip.

I have a little jar of Chimayo earth. Chimayo is a town near Santa Fe. In the church there, off to one side of the altar, in a sacristy, is a little well that goes down into the earth. A lot of people come there to get a handful of that earth. I suppose many people do that, non-Indians as well as Indians. They've heard about it because it has a certain magical quality. I call it a healing earth. I put some Chimayo earth in my mixture, my magic.

Meeting Before the Hard Distance: Pathways

When I was discharged from Gillette Children's Hospital after my hip operation, I came home. I was limited, but I was able to get around pretty well.

I suppose I felt different, after picking up slang and getting out into the world, broader than just the little village where I was brought up.

Chippewa City as I knew it is gone now, but Grand Marais looks much the same as I remember, though it is spread out, north, south, west. The East Bay Hotel used to be the Sterling Hotel. We picked raspberries with my father on Maple Hill and sold them to Mrs. Sterling. Ten cents a quart, Depression prices. But that was good money because for a water pail full of berries, you'd get a buck twenty. That was about twelve quarts. Two of us could each carry two full pails. We got a lot of berries when the season was on.

Mrs. Sterling was quite a woman. Apparently her husband had died, or they had separated. She took over the hotel herself. She must have been energetic and enterprising. She did the cooking, she did everything, though I'm sure she had help.

What is now Joynes Department Store and Ben Franklin Store was Peter Alm's store. Howard Joynes, who was a couple years ahead of me in school, worked for him. The store was across from the Blue Water Cafe, where the parking lot is now. Howard was Alm's protégé of sorts; he bought the store before Pete Alm died. He made it his own, then he incorporated it with the Ben

1 9 2 9 – 1 9 4 3

Grand Marais in the
1920s and 1930s

The Witch Tree

High school

Minneapolis
School of Art

Influential teachers

One year at home

Beginnings of
artistic development

Graduation with
scholarship to New York

Franklin company. We kidded him because he was getting to be sort of a shrewd business person. Even now, we call him Howard Franklin or Ben Joynes.

In those days we didn't know that the Witch Tree existed. Though it's become quite known now, I don't think even the Grand Portage people knew about it then, except for a very few. An artist, Dewey Albinson, came up here in the 1930s and '40s, as I understand. He was a rugged individual and painted in a realistic way, rugged, expressionistic but realistic. He painted portraits of some of the older Grand Portage residents. He also painted the Witch Tree; he helped name the tree and made it better known through his painting.

The Indians called it Ma-ni-do Gee-zhi-gance, or Spirit Little Cedar Tree. Hazel uses that name in her paintings. I'm not in favor of the name Witch Tree because I don't think the tree has any of the bad connotation of witch-es. Yet it is old and has survived in a unique way. I've heard stories that even the early French explorers stopped to pay reverence to it for a safe journey.

As I grew up, I started to buy my own clothes. As soon as I was aware of myself in high school, I wanted to look neat and proper. I began to get odd jobs in town or for private people.

Grand Marais, ca. 1910.

Minnesota Historical Society

When I started back to school, I continued to make illustrations for the town kids. They gave me swaps; that's how I acquired more than one jack-knife. I was always fiddling around, whittling with a jackknife, doing something with my hands.

You know how tourists buy trinkets? I made little bow-and-arrows, tie racks with a canoe theme. Then I painted designs, arbitrarily red to make them attractive. I'd make them out of cedar, carve them, get them all nice and rounded with the jackknife, then sand them. Oh, they were attractive.

Little tomahawks, too. I used to get a stone that was shaped right, then tie it with some rawhide that was lying around the house. If you apply it wet, the rawhide dries and tightens up so it holds the rock onto the handle. I used to paint red designs on the rocks. Maybe I'd get a dollar for those.

I bought a sweater when I was in high school. It might have cost four or five dollars, which was a lot of money in those days. I thought it was a very special sweater. I remember it was blue. Why? I don't know.

When I was going into high school, other Indian boys were in demand as athletes for the school, for basketball primarily. I don't think we had a football team. Maybe I could have played basketball. In my situation, I couldn't be a powerful runner, but it was possible that I could have played basketball, yes. Having a lame leg made me very shy. Otherwise, I might have been more out-going, playing ball, being part of a team.

The high school principal was also our English teacher, a good one. She made us aware of literature as an art. We read Dickens. *Oliver Twist, David Copperfield.*

I was pretty green about a lot of things. I didn't know what art was all about, even though I knew how to draw. You don't realize the vastness of art until you begin to experience your own life, and then stories that relate to your life, and what other artists and authors are doing in regard to their work, writing about their own times and their own experience.

"It was the best of times, it was the worst of times." That famous line from *A Tale of Two Cities*. Those contrasts help make even young readers like myself enjoy reading Dickens. I think one reason he was so popular is that he dealt with different levels of society, playing up the idea of success, coming out of the muck and becoming successful.

The kids I swapped with were not my friends. There were very few people in my class that I became close to. One was a young boy from Lutsen, Don McCall; he was one of my school chums. We always skipped school together.

Since he came from way above Lutsen, he had to walk to the main road to catch the bus. He used to show me a lead bullet that he got from a deer he had shot. He started out young, living off the land, hunting and trapping.

I don't know what his father did, or his mother, or what their background was. I was never at his house. He was smart and so was his brother Hamilton. Like me, he was in the middle of our class of thirty-five, which was a big class for that day.

I was pretty good in some subjects like history and geography and not so good at chemistry or other sciences. Don and I were not dumb, but we were not absolutely smart like Florence Gunderson. Florence was our valedictorian.

Some people say "book smart." But I think Florence was more than that.

When we were kids in Chippewa City, there were roads, slower and rougher than those today, but no one had a car. We had a lot of distant relatives in Grand Portage. We saw them only occasionally when they came to Grand Marais or we went to Grand Portage. The steamer *America* was the prime mover of people up and down the lake shore. It stopped in Tofte, at Grand Marais, at Hovland.

I never went on it.

Discrimination—yes, I felt that. There were always bound to be some who were more belligerent in putting down the Indians. There were a few of those boys around. I don't know how the girls felt.

I recall some incidents when the put-downs amounted to scrapping. Nothing vicious. But it would not encourage you to take part in school activities.

A teacher named Clark was in Grand Marais for only a couple of years as a manual training instructor, for shop work, woodworking, and illustrations like technical drawing. I think he liked me, for one thing because I was Indian. We had a kind of rapport. I was good at manual training, good with my hands, and good at certain kinds of illustration. I could whiz through those things like nothing. He liked me for that. He gave me A+.

I made a chair in manual training. It might have been modern for the time. I got the blueprints from somewhere. I followed them, and the chair came out of that plan.

When the WPA came in during the Depression, I got a job in the high school library mending books. Six dollars a month—it was a very helping kind of wage for a young kid.

George (right) with the chair he built in a manual training class taught by Donald Clark (second from right), Grand Marais High School, ca. 1937.

Courtesy of George Morrison

Indian CCC camp at Grand Portage, 1937.
Minnesota Historical Society
(W. M. Babcock)

We didn't help support the family. The money we earned was more or less for ourselves—in my case, buying my own clothes or my own treats. Another neighbor boy my age played a guitar. My uncle had a violin. I bought a guitar, a mandolin, and a banjo. I used to play those instruments by ear.

We played together with this friend of mine. Someone else would play a harmonica. We used to have a lot of fun, playing with a group of people who wanted to dance or sing.

High school dances were more formal; I was too shy for them. I didn't mingle too much with the crowd at large.

When I was seventeen, I got into a CCC camp for Indians in Grand Portage. Indian boys came from around the state and were paid about thirty dollars a month. That was standard pay for CCC boys.

One year I worked in the kitchen. Then I worked outside in the woods. Foresters were the foremen and told us what to do. We spent every day pulling up small trees that were beginning to be diseased. Could have been white pine that got blister rust. We pulled them out of the ground so the disease wouldn't spread.

It was just a mundane job, but it was good healthy work. It helped create good rapport with different Indians from all over. We stayed in a barracks and ate in a communal dining room. There was a good baseball team, which was fun.

My hunting was practically none. I wasn't a woods person like some of my brothers. I never shot a deer. I've been hunting but I was never able to see an animal and shoot it.

My father hunted but he was not always successful either. Sometimes you have hunter's luck: You go out all day and don't get anything.

We did maple sugaring, certainly. Every family in Chippewa City had a certain part of the sugar bush, where they set up camp for making sugar, as they did for trapping. I guess sugaring was dying out by the time I was in high school.

My English teacher encouraged people to consider going to college. Mrs. Hal Downey, a neighbor in Chippewa City (they had a summer home on the lake), also encouraged me. She liked me because I was one of the few finishing school, then going on to study art. I considered enrolling in commercial art as a means of making a living. I had certain talents in art, using my hands. Art school would fit what I wanted to do. My English teacher helped identify the Minneapolis School of Art , then associated with the Minneapolis Institute of Arts. It was the only art school in the area.

In 1938 after I graduated high school, I entered the Minneapolis School of Art. With some loans from the Consolidated Chippewa Indian Agency and, along the way, some scholarships from the school, I was always lucky enough to get tuition paid.

For school I bought a new paint box. In those days, paint boxes were little, like attaché cases. Little wooden boxes to hold paint sets and brushes.

I probably traveled to the Twin Cities by Greyhound bus. My clothes were very plain. As I remember, I wore a brown suit. I probably didn't take my

George (left) and fellow students at the Minneapolis School of Art, ca. 1940.

Courtesy of George Morrison

guitar, at least not this first trip; maybe later, in a pillowcase. I didn't have a regular case for it.

Coming from a small town, I was pretty green moving into a big city. I didn't know many people. But gradually I made my way into the dominant society, going to art school, having talent, competing with other kids. Taking up art was a lot of fun—it was good for me.

The art school directed me to some boarding and rooming houses close by. I stayed at Smiths' rooming house and ate at a boarding house a few blocks away. They were all near the art school.

As time progressed, I ran out of loan money and scholarship money, so I began sharing an apartment with other students; we did our own cooking.

We always walked to save the dime for trolley fare. "Walking distance" meant six or eight blocks, which was nothing. We even walked downtown, which was quite a walk.

George (standing) at the Smiths' rooming house, Minneapolis, 1938.

Courtesy of George Morrison

At first, because I started in commercial art, I took advertising. There were a lot of design courses and color courses. Color came naturally to me. I fell right into it; I did well.

There were also basic classes, the drawing courses that everyone took, like drawing from the nude, for instance. They had a nude model on a model stand, and all the students, maybe twenty-five in all, sat in the round, drawing the model. That was a pretty standard thing, learning how to draw a figure.

Everybody did much the same thing. Everybody drew the figure. And everyone's figure was pretty much the same.

From that time at art school, there are only a few of my paintings still in existence. One is a portrait, fairly realistic; I called it *Dirt Track Specialist*.

It's done in profile, with a palette knife, but very fine, exacting work. Not a slick painting like the kind the academics were teaching. They were very

Dirt Track Specialist, ca. 1940
Oil on canvas
24 x 20
Collection Hazel Belvo

slick. I guess certain students, including myself, were reacting against the academicism.

Academic painting prevailed, a continuous line from the nineteenth century right into the twentieth. As part of the standard academic treatment, we all varnished our paintings. I remember we used spray varnish. You put it in a little blower and then blew it from the bottle. The spray came out to freshen up the canvas.

The man in the portrait was a model, an older man posing in a sulky outfit—he's wearing the cap and scarf of sulky drivers at the State Fair. That's where the "Dirt Track" comes from. But the "Specialist" is mine.

When I was growing up, being able to draw and carve things was strictly the physical part of making something. But during my art school years, I was beginning to find out that art was a very broad endeavor. This so-called creating something had broad meaning.

I went to libraries, looked at real art in the museum, and read books on art; I was beginning to find out what I liked. We used to have lectures once a week on art history, from the old masters to the present day. I had a tendency to like more modern concepts. But I appreciated the old.

In 1939 the art institute had a big retrospective of Picasso. I was very impressed. Certainly a lot of people were trying to figure it out. It was very extreme for Minneapolis. Picasso's exaggeration, his distortion of color, took people by surprise. Yet, you know, it wasn't complete abstraction.

After the first few years of art school, I switched out of commercial art to fine arts. Now I studied drawing and painting.

I suppose I was influenced by the seriousness of being an artist and all the romance connected with it. I don't mean romance in a corny sense, but in a broad artistic sense. Romantic—it's a broad term. I probably had a romantic notion of playing the role of the artist, living in a garret, being poor, trying to survive as an artist. I thought about that but I didn't glorify it.

I was becoming more radical, more individual. I was showing a special talent in the class. I chummed around with some of the talented upper-level kids, too. You know, I always looked up to those kids who got the big scholarships. Even before I came to art school, I had read about them in the school bulletin. When I was starting, they were seniors, the big shots at school.

As it turned out, I got scholarships myself. In 1942 a scholarship from the Woman's Club of Minneapolis paid my full tuition. The teachers selected me.

To start with, I spent time strictly on school. Later, I worked at a bowling alley where leagues played in the evenings. My job was to sweep a wide dusting broom up one alley and down the next. I did that between the bowling tournaments to keep the alleys dust-free.

It was a good job. I ate there; it was a combination restaurant and bowling alley. I knew the family who managed it. They were Jewish, and the mother, who was getting on in years, was the cook. The daughter was in art school with me. We weren't really friends; she took other subjects than I did. She was also a little stuck-up. She probably wouldn't have bothered with me.

I was still rather shy, but I made good friends in art school. My friends were good students, too.

My mother never knew how to write, but my sister Mary, who stayed home to help raise the children and keep house, helped my mother write. That was my connection to home, a lot of letters with gossip, mundane news.

Then I went home summers.

After my first year at art school, I had a second operation to help me walk straighter. It helped but it was a crude method compared to those today, when they give you brand new hips made of plastic and steel.

My initial operation as a boy at Gillette Hospital had left me with a crippled leg. I was able to walk but my left leg didn't grow as fast as my right leg. That made me more self-conscious.

Now I was in a cast on both legs up to my waist to keep them immobile. I was in the hospital for several months, then I took the rest of the year off from school and came home to Chippewa City.

It was always good to come home and see my family. At the same time, I was anxious to get back to school and resume the art thing. I was developing my own ideas about what I wanted to be, even thinking about New York. So I must have felt a little apart from the others in the family, a little more advanced or educated.

I wanted to be serious; I brought my paint box and paints home. I was playing the role of the artist a little, painting landscapes. I recall doing about fifty canvases a year. Some were saved by my family; others I stored in a rooming house when I graduated and left for New York. Eventually, they were lost. I wish I had some of them now.

One of the few paintings that remains was bought by the Minneapolis Institute of Arts. It is called *Mt. Maude.* I painted it outside with an easel, in the old, so-called romantic way of doing things—*plein air* depiction.

I was home for the summer, staying with my brother Bernard at his forestry tower on Mt. Maud. That was near what used to be Mineral Center, a little community on top of the hill above Grand Portage, four or five miles up. Bernard was married by then, with children, and they lived in a cabin at the foot of the tower. You had to walk up a steep, sloping hill to the base of the tower. He climbed the tower to do his job, watching for fires.

I must have been very glad to make fifty bucks selling *Mt. Maude* to the art institute. It was purchased from the Local Art Purchase Fund, out of the institute's Annual Local Artists' Exhibition. All the students were interested in trying to show as much as they could; I was fortunate to get in that one.

I probably painted it in an afternoon, setting up my easel on the ground and adjusting it so I could stand at it. I used a palette and an oil paint box,

standard equipment for art students. I worked by observation, looking at the subject matter in front of me—the mountains, the grasses, the trees and winding road, and lots of goldenrod along the road. Then I depicted it, modifying it to a certain degree. You always arrange the composition as you go along.

At that time, I was into painting in the Regionalist manner. This was during the 1930s and '40s when that style was very popular. Painters like

Mt. Maude, ca. 1942
Oil on canvas
26 x 32
Collection Minneapolis Institute of Arts

Grant Wood, John Steuart Curry, and Thomas Hart Benton were each associated with a particular area: Wood with Iowa, Curry with Kansas, and Benton with Missouri. Benton was considered radical because of his exaggerated forms and brushstrokes, though his works still illustrated a subject. Under their influence, my own brushstrokes were beginning to be expressionistic.

At art school, a couple of teachers stand out in my memory. Alexander Masley was one. He had graduated from the Minneapolis School of Art and gone on to study in Chicago and New York. Probably at the Institute of Design in Chicago, an offshoot of the Bauhaus in Germany. The Bauhaus, one of the foremost schools in Europe, taught advanced principles in art. Some of the teachers escaped the Nazis and came to this country.

Masley was brilliant and picked up a lot of new ideas. I was one of the many students impressed by him. He was instrumental in shaping my ideas, as opposed to other, more academic teachers. They followed the very exacting, old academic ways. Masley wasn't like that. He encouraged more open experiment, more freedom, more individual expression. That was right up my alley.

Another teacher instrumental in my development was Frances Greenman—a well-known portrait painter in her day, in the style of John Singer Sargent. I remember seeing one of her portraits, possibly the *Red-Headed Boy,* hanging at the art institute. At the art school she was asked to teach still life, even though she was a portrait painter. I think the other portrait teachers taught in the academic style, which she did not work in.

Her class was standard still-life study as a means of getting the shapes of objects and the character of a table or vase. She liked doing still lifes and emphasized setting up different textures—a tablecloth, pitchers, glassware, candlesticks. We saw seventeenth-century Dutch still lifes in the institute, and those of Cézanne and the Impressionists. Cézanne and Renoir were regarded as more extreme, even though their works were fifty or so years old by then. You might say this country is always fifty or a hundred years behind the avant-garde.

As a teacher, Frances Greenman was close to her students, very friendly towards us. Like most teachers today, she exchanged anecdotes and critiques and gave little suggestions from her own process.

She became friends with an older woman who was taking classes there. This woman was from southwestern Minnesota, possibly LeSueur; she came from a wealthy family that may have owned the Minnesota Valley Canning Company. Frances Greenman had done a portrait of someone in her family. The two women were quite friendly with all of us; we even went down to the woman's home as guests. It made the students, including me, feel more important.

We also had little parties together, and Frances Greenman introduced us to the sociability of drinking—she liked cocktails, martinis, and such things. My own association with drinking from my environment had been kind of raw. When we were kids, we used to buy a big bottle of beer and share it, then hide it in the woods. It wasn't social drinking; that didn't exist in the village. It was cruder, with a bottle on the table or maybe in the hip pocket, then drinking right out of the bottle.

I analyze it this way. A lot of Indians are inclined to be silent, and very shy. Then when they have a few drinks, they loosen up a bit, begin to talk more, even do dancing, or jigging. I think they became more quiet because they were pushed almost underground. The Indian race was here first; then came the tremendous advance of western expansion.

Andrew Jackson, for example, was like Hitler. His idea for solving the "Indian problem" was to get rid of them, kill them off. A lot of Indians did their best to defend themselves, their land, and their ideas. Major Indian wars were fought up and down the East Coast from as early as King Philip's War in New England in the 1670s.

George (left) with art school
classmates Jim Caldwell and
Alfred Brunettin, ca. 1940.

Courtesy of George Morrison

Then 160 years later when Jackson became president, he removed the Cherokee along the Trail of Tears to Oklahoma. The Cherokee were a tremendous nation; they had developed a strong culture. When they were forced to leave their homeland in the Carolinas and Georgia, a lot of them died. It was like moving animals.

It's pretty remarkable that, pushed as they were, the various tribes survived. I think that their strong art and philosophies gave the people strength. You can't kill that.

World War II started when I was in art school. Recently I was reading an account of Eleanor Roosevelt and remembered that we knew she was for pacifism. In art school, liberal factions rallied to try and keep us out of the war. I did my bit, I suppose, passing out literature.

My good friend from high school, Don McCall, was killed in the war. Another good friend in art school that I used to room with, Jim Caldwell, was a navigator on a B-17 that was shot down.

I also knew a lot of men, some relatives from Grand Portage, who got into the war. I think that Indians, by inheriting certain characteristics of warrior societies, were ready and able to go to war.

I could have been shot up, too, if it wasn't for my leg. That's how I always look at it.

Lots of us art students were beginning to look to New York, the art capital of the world. For a long time Paris had been the capital, but that had shifted to the New World right at the time that I was going to art school. Many European artists emigrated because of the Nazi repression and then the war. I had dreamed of going to New York, to the Art Students League; that was a big deal at art school. Where did you go? You went to New York.

Luckily, when I graduated from the Minneapolis School of Art in 1943, I received the Ethel Morrison Van Derlip scholarship to continue my studies. It was the highest honor in the school. In those days they split the scholarships among the top talents. It was shared, but it was still an honor to get it.

My mother came down for graduation. Things were letting up from the Depression. I don't know how she got the money to come down, but she did.

She separated from my father, too, around this time and moved to Duluth. I don't know the reasons—incompatibility or whatever. It wasn't a shock; we sensed it all along. My father was not abusive in the sense that he beat his wife, but he was alcoholic. He didn't drink every day like some alcoholics. He sometimes made good money by trapping. But he would sometimes lose that money by drinking or being robbed, not really tending to his family as he should.

That was the environment in which I grew up. There was some violence in the village and there was a lot of alcoholism. Whenever alcohol was available, whenever the people who drank had money to spend on it, they would drink.

On her own, my mother had kind of a struggle. I think she had a little help from some of my brothers. Eventually she met another man and it worked out okay. But at first it was a struggle.

After graduation, I came home for the summer and worked at odd jobs to earn money. Then in the fall I took the train to New York.

The trains were full of soldiers. There were restrictions on traveling because of the war. You had to have a certain kind of pass to ride the train; I guess they did that for security reasons.

I took one suitcase. I don't even remember if I carried art materials; if so, it was probably the paint box I had bought when I first went to art school. I had very limited luggage.

EXTENDED PATH: VIOLET WATER

I went by train, tourist class. It was a big deal for me, traveling to New York. When the train arrived in Penn Station, I might have checked my brown hat and suitcase or I might have taken them with me directly to the Art Students League. I don't remember.

The League was housed in a big building from the 1870s or '80s, four or five stories high. It was on 57th Street between Seventh and Eighth avenues, in what they now call the Upper West Side. The office gave me some places to look for a room, and I found one in Hell's Kitchen on the West Side.

After checking into the room, I remember walking down toward Times Square. I was very impressed by the lights of the big city, interested to be on the scene. On later trips, especially when I approached New York at night, it looked like a magical city—bridges and all of Manhattan lit up like a magical place. Always impressive. I still get the same charge when I approach it.

Meeting the other students, again I was impressed. Cicely Aikman was one of the first students I met. Cicely and I became friendly and later romantic. She was tall and angular, not a conventional beauty, but smart-looking in her own way. Her family was educated—her father in the diplomatic corps, her mother a graduate of Smith College. I visited them a few times in Washington. They were liberal enough to appreciate her going to art school.

1943–1952

Art Students League

Living and working
in New York

Changes in painting style

Summers at
Provincetown and
Cape Ann

Group shows in
small galleries

First solo show at
Grand Central Moderns

Marriage to Ada Reed

At the beginning I had a German instructor. I didn't like him even though he was pretty well known. He was too businesslike; his work was rigid, too. So I looked in the catalog and read about Morris Kantor. He sounded liberal, and I liked his reproductions. So I moved over to his class. Kantor was not an abstractionist, not yet anyway. That came later. The term you could use for his work was romantic Expressionist. One of the more liberal teachers, Kantor was radical compared to some of the other instructors.

Kantor's class is where I met Cicely and also Harry Sexton, from New Jersey. Harry had a big red nose and glasses; he was kind of nervous, but he had a good talent and I appreciated that. He had a unique style of painting, working very much by himself, putting on his strokes in a very personal way. He went through a clown period, doing Harlequin figures—careful, but well done.

Cicely, who was friends with both of us, was more experimental and expressionistic. She worked from the model, then scratched it out and painted over it again. Very, very experimental, with the figure visible but marked over with paint.

I had begun to experiment in art school in Minneapolis. Sometimes I painted three paintings on one canvas, one on one side, one on the other side, then a third on top of the first, letting the original come through. Making best use of the canvas and not worrying whether it was going to be good or saving it for posterity. Just working, gaining experience with the paint again and again. All part of the expression of the age.

Jumping from Minneapolis to New York and meeting those radical students like me, I felt very free. We were doing what we wanted to do.

Of course, as I talked to students, I found factions at the League. The League varied from one aesthetic extreme to the other. Some students followed Frank DuMond, an old realist from way back. He was a respected teacher of a sugary realism, very academic. We used to put his students down by calling them "DuMond students." Yet we knew some of these guys and argued our differences. Another teacher was Yasuo Kuniyoshi, a Japanese American. He used a little exaggeration in an illustrative way. There was no abstraction at the League yet. That crept in toward the 1950s.

One of the modern extremists was Vaclav Vytlacil. His work touched on abstraction but still kept figurative elements. A lot of the so-called radical students, who were close to me as friends, were students of his.

Kantor came twice a week to the League, probably Tuesdays and Thursdays. As I remember, our class was held on the fourth floor; the building was a walk-up, no elevator. Kantor also taught at Cooper Union. A lot of students came to the Art Students League from Cooper Union, all smart kids, Jewish kids and mixtures of different nationalities. When they found out about me, they kidded me about the "Indian bit." They didn't do it derogatorily; it was all in kidding, so it was OK. I didn't worry about fitting in. I was where I wanted to be.

When classes were over, we often went around the corner to Carney's pub. Kantor liked to eat with the students. We could have beer or whatever we wanted. Then we would decide on a place for dinner somewhere in Manhattan. It was always a nice thing. Gradually I picked up on different ethnic foods, Greek or Chinese. One of our favorite places was Chinatown. That was the best Chinese food in America outside of San Francisco.

When Kantor wasn't at the League, a monitor named Phyllis Goldstein, who was also a student, took charge of the model and of attendance. It wasn't that strict. People could come and go; it was pretty free. By and large, the kids were serious and stuck to their guns. They went every day to paint.

To work from the model, each of us had a bench, just a plain box with a front where you placed a drawing board with paper tacked onto it. Then you straddled the bench. All the students would group around the model stand, at angles for comfortable viewing and working.

One of our regular models often dressed in biblical dress. We called him Sea of Galilee. He was a good model, very sincere, a kind person, very feminine but not in a bad way. He made his own costumes from things he picked up and then elaborated on. He was available all over New York City, at Cooper Union, different colleges. He'd get up on the stand, people would say, "Pose, please," and he would hold the pose for twenty-five minutes. He knew how.

Untitled (Nude female on back), 1944
Ink on paper
11½ x 9
Collection Tweed Museum of Art,
University of Minnesota, Duluth
Gift of the artist

It was strictly classroom work. I was beginning to use the model more as a departure, incorporating it into paintings that had other elements. This was broadening the concept of painting beyond simple portraiture as I'd practiced it in *Dirt Track Specialist* from my Minneapolis days. Now I was beginning to stretch the model into a symbol, making up things in my head.

After I was established at school a few months, I decided to get an apartment in Greenwich Village with Harry Sexton. We found one for $30 a month on Waverly Place in the center of the Village. Pretty cheap for an apartment with heat—it was a third-floor walk-up, essentially a cold-water flat.

Cicely also lived in the Village around the same time, sharing a large apartment with three or four others, some of whom had taken classes at the League, others who were getting started as secretaries. There was a group of them in this large apartment, very nice, right off Washington Square.

You always think of the Village as being a quaint place, going to the park in Washington Square, meeting a few characters, buying vegetables and fruits from the carts of Italian vendors on Bleecker Street. Lots of artists and art students lived in the Village. It was a nice place to be.

At the same time, it was kind of a jungle—all industrial, with old and abandoned factories. Bums were around; I met a few. They were harmless. They used to inhabit big cartons abandoned on the street.

To get up to the Art Students League, we hopped a subway. I probably carried my paint box from the Minneapolis days, and I took my sketchbook with me everywhere. It was around 12 by 14 inches. I was more attached to the sketchbook than some other art students. I sketched people in the subway; I sketched models at the League. We had dancers, nudes. Nudity is a part of art. Think about the work of Michelangelo or Botticelli's *Birth of Venus* in the Uffizi in Florence.

This is the century of Expressionism. That's the way I see it. It started at the turn of the century, around 1905 in Europe with the Fauves and Picasso's Rose and Blue periods, his Harlequin families and other work. Then it came into

Untitled (Man leaning on arm),
1943
Ink and pencil on paper
7½ x 5
Collection Tweed Museum of Art,
University of Minnesota, Duluth
Gift of the artist

this country with the Armory Show in 1913. Expressionism kept right on going into the 1920s and 1930s with Cubism and Surrealism. When I arrived in New York, it was full-blossomed.

During the war a lot of emigres came from Europe to escape the Nazis. They came primarily to New York. Many were Jewish; a lot were from Estonia, France, Italy. The galleries along 57th Street were full of the Surrealism and Expressionism they brought with them.

When we wanted to escape the cafeteria food at the Art Students League, Harry and I and the other kids often ate along 57th Street, the street of galleries. We were always going into galleries and running around town to museums. We'd hop on a subway or a bus and go all over the city for a dime. We could easily take a bus from the League to the Metropolitan Museum of Art.

We also often went to the Museum of Modern Art to see their permanent collection. One or two of Picasso's Harlequins were there. I've seen the paintings so many times that they have become like old friends. I want to see them again and again.

The popular American art of the day, the Americana style, still existed but it was fading. Thomas Hart Benton, for instance, had come to New York and, by chance, taught Jackson Pollock, who had arrived from Wyoming. (It wasn't a big deal in the sense that Benton made Pollock an artist; Pollock just took some courses from him.) Pollock went on to develop Abstract Expressionism, a combination of Cubism and Surrealism that crept into abstraction. As I arrived on the scene, this shift was just beginning.

During 1945 I did a number of paintings and drawings with three figures. Sometimes three figures that merged into two. The compositions evolved through the process of drawing and painting. It was all very subconscious. A kind of dreamlike Surrealism creeping in. They were somber works, with dark colors and the beginnings of Expressionism in exaggerated, elongated figures.

You could analyze it this way: I had started an affair with Cicely Aikman. She had been going with a Jewish boy. Then he left for the armed services in Europe. Our romance was frustrating because she felt guilty about her former boyfriend. She wanted to be true to him, and at the same time she was torn

Three Figures, 1945
Gouache and ink on paper
11⅜ x 8½
Collection Minnesota Museum
of American Art
Gift of the artist

about being alone. I was there, pushing for us. Our relationship lasted until he returned from the war, after 1945 or '46. So the paintings contain the symbolism of three people; one of them is me.

I couldn't have done work like this in Minneapolis. In Minneapolis the teachers were pushing a certain kind of realism; they were portrait painters.

They wouldn't have gone in for this at all. This was the influence of New York; this was going toward Expressionism.

Paintings like *Juxtaposition* also had elements of Cubism. I juxtaposed elements within the figures—the bust, the stomach, the thighs. I also based a number of works on a model who was a dancer. She did some Martha Graham kind of dancing all over our big studio. I made quick sketches, then paintings came out of them, with the symbolism of two or three figures again.

When I left home in 1943, I bought a one-way ticket to New York. Then I wrote simple letters home, describing my fascination with the city, my first observations. No telephones. Letter writing was the only contact. My father, who knew how to write, never wrote; the other kids wrote for my mother.

Juxtaposition, 1945–1946
Oil on canvas
32 x 26
Location unknown
Photo courtesy of George Morrison

I guess I was still attached to my parents, and I was lonesome that first year. So I came home the following summer. I don't think I stayed very long, and I don't think I worked once I was there. I'm not even sure if my parents had divorced by that time or not. I just remember eating and sleeping at home.

That summer I showed a portrait at the Minnesota State Fair and won third place in the ribbon awards, no cash. The Grand Marais paper said I was "in the cities" for the summer, painting portraits of prominent people. I don't know how true that was. I wasn't really a portrait painter.

Back in New York in the fall of 1944, starting my second year at the League, I was awarded the Bernays scholarship for continued study. Kantor was good about recommending me for tuition scholarships, but he'd

say, "If you want a letter, you write it and I'll sign it." He was that kind of guy. Cicely or someone else would help me write a letter. We all helped each other.

I began to be involved in group shows and occasionally sold a piece. A group of us would get together and buy big sheets of plywood or Masonite, cut it up in sections and paint on surfaces that we had gessoed first. I sometimes stretched canvas over small square or rectangular shapes called stretchers. We were after the cheapest materials possible, going together to buy in bulk, any way to make ends meet.

We used to kid around with big titles for those paintings. "Arrival and Departure," Harry Sexton would say. Maybe that was a title of a novel from the time. Harry was punning and having a good time.

I had started working at a frame shop nearby run by a former Kantor student named Carl Ashby, from Utah. His shop had one room that served as a gallery where we all showed at one time or another. It was possible to buy ads in the *Herald Tribune* or the *New York Times,* one-inch ads for maybe $30 or $40. We might do that, or advertise in the local paper called the *Villager* for less money.

We would sell from those shows. I remember selling small paintings for ten bucks. Of course, ten bucks was more then than it is today. A good ten bucks. I suppose it would be comparable today for a student in art school to sell a canvas for $100 or $150.

Some of us also worked at a button factory painting buttons—one of the many jobs we students got for quick money. The factory was in the so-called Garment District on the West Side. I think it was a fly-by-night shop. They wanted us to paint the buttons fast so they could get more for their money. The designs we painted may have been copied from something else. It was my first production-line job and also my first experience with a union, which I joined. I liked hand-painting the fancy buttons. Our motto: "Make a good button but make it fast!"

My second summer in New York, instead of going home, I made my way to Provincetown on the tip of Cape Cod. It was closer than Minnesota, and student friends at the League had gone there and liked it. The population of three thousand in the Portuguese fishing village swelled during the summer with all the artists and tourists. It had a nice feel to it.

With its harbor, Provincetown is a lot like Grand Marais—Lake Superior, the Atlantic Ocean, the big waters. Indians call Lake Superior Chi-goo-mee, the big water, because it is the biggest water in mid-America. One of the common spellings is Gitchi Gumee. But Indians don't say the "Gitchi." They say "Chi-goo-mee." "Chi" means big, and "goo-mee" means water.

There is a different feel to different bodies of water. With the Atlantic, the color of the water is grayer and greener and the waves longer. They say on the North Shore, here on Lake Superior, you can see seven miles to the edge. Beyond that is something else.

Provincetown took to me right away. I was very impressed by it, the flavor of the town, the pristine light reflecting off the ocean, the climate, the water. I have an affinity for water, big water. I have always felt good being near the water because of being born right near the lake.

Cape Cod is a big curve, and Provincetown is way out at the tip. In Provincetown you can go to beaches on the ocean side and also on the bay side where the town is. Lots of places for swimming.

I became fascinated by beach-combing and found objects there. I liked walking along the different beaches in Provincetown—the ocean side, the bay side—finding all kinds of interesting objects

Starfish (Starfish and Whalebone), 1945
Oil on canvas
26 x 32
Location unknown
Photo courtesy of George Morrison

that might have been cast away from ships, including pieces of wood. The curiosity I'd had as a kid in Grand Marais—finding cast-off wood or toys, using butcher knives to whittle and carve—carried over, I suppose, to the beaches in Provincetown. Things I found on the beach I took home—a starfish, a whalebone. Interesting shapes and textures that I used in my paintings.

Provincetown was fairly accessible to New York; that's another reason I went. Otherwise, I would have gone home that second summer, as I had the first.

With another student friend from New York, Martin Bloom, I found jobs in Provincetown. I remember dishwashing in a restaurant for a while and working on construction jobs, helping the carpenters. Not really carpentry, just hauling lumber and such.

Martin had graduated from Cooper Union, where Morris Kantor also taught, and then like a lot of other Cooper Union students, he came to take classes at the Art Students League, wanting to develop his art just as I did.

Martin and I rented a garage converted into living quarters. Upstairs was an apartment and downstairs was an apartment—not really apartments, just open spaces with facilities for sleeping and cooking. We may have paid a hundred bucks a season each.

The rents in Provincetown were cheaper than New York, and we cooked at home—you don't eat out so much in a small place like that. Eating out in big cities is a big thing. Later I began washing dishes in a restaurant called the Seascape. They liked me, and the next summer they gave me board and room at the back, next to the place where they did their laundry.

When World War II ended, an interesting thing happened. A tremendous influx of students came back from the war, many to the Art Students League. They brought back their experiences of foreign places in Europe and the Pacific. At the same time younger people like Robert Rauschenberg were beginning to study at the League, developing their own kind of Expressionism. Rauschenberg's work has touches of Surrealism, overlapping ideas like collage and photomontage, and tricks in the imagery.

During the school year I worked at the frame shop run by Carl Ashby. Carl was tall and lanky, a little older than I, very intelligent and knowledgeable about art, and also very handy with frames. I was handy, too; frame-making came easy for me. I made a fairly decent hourly wage. The shop was at 18 Cornelia Street near West Fourth Street and Sixth Avenue. It was also near my apartment in Greenwich Village. I worked at the frame shop a number of years, part-time, full-time; it was my prime money-making in New York.

In a little gallery that developed at the shop, a number of us who studied with Kantor and knew or worked for Carl formed the Pyramid Group around 1945. Helen De Mott, a New Yorker; Cicely Aikman, Phyllis Goldstein, and Harry Sexton, my friends from Kantor's class; Martin Bloom, my roommate from Provincetown; Louie Finkelstein, a leader of the group, very verbal. We were all young artists with the same goals, pursuing our painting and working at menial jobs. We did everything together, meeting in each other's studios—we called them studios, but they were really just big spaces for living and working. When it came time to plan shows, we all took equal division of the planning and work. We had enough talent and variety to warrant showing.

One of my first shows at the Ashby Gallery was in 1946 with Phyllis Goldstein and a Japanese-American painter named Kazumi Sonoda. Ashby wrote a foreword in the catalog: "That New York is the focal point of art activity in the country is evidenced somewhat by this show. Kazumi Sonoda from Alameda, Cal., George Morrison from Minneapolis, and Phyllis Goldstein of New York are all at present working here, each in an individual manner, yet all in an expressionist vein."

Ashby was intelligent enough to show all the Pyramid Group, including himself; he gave younger artists a chance to display their work. His gallery became a meeting place for the group and for our shows.

The Pyramid Group also jumped around to different places. For example, "The Eye and the Lens," which was "a show of paintings with photos of the subjects that inspired them," featured works by twenty-two of us at the Pyramid Gallery, 59 East Eighth Street. One of the artists had a loft at that address where we occasionally showed. Later we showed at the Riverside Museum, a

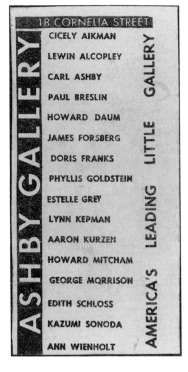

Ashby Gallery advertisement, ca. 1946.

Morrison scrapbook

very obscure, out-of-the-way museum on the Upper West Side at Riverside Drive and 103rd Street. They did offbeat shows, including the Pyramid Group's.

A lot of us were encouraged to be part of the hanging of these shows. Usually the people who did the hanging would put themselves in a prominent place. So you wanted to be there to make sure you weren't hung off in the corner.

There were groups popping up all over New York during these decades of the '40s and '50s. They were part of the gallery system, as I see it now. We all had little followings, people who would come to see us in out-of-the-way places. And we didn't have to force the press to attend. They came on their own. Bigger galleries attracted bigger names and probably had bigger space in the press. We often got only a mention. But that was a good start. It was a big deal to be mentioned by the *Times*.

In 1946, my last year at the League, I was fortunate to get into some big shows—at the Whitney Museum of American Art in New York and the Pennsylvania Academy of the Fine Arts. I entered and got in, competing with national figures. It was one way to break into the art world.

I also had work exhibited at the Woman's Club in Minneapolis. The headline for John K. Sherman's *Minneapolis Star-Journal* article read, "Surrealist Ranks Swell at Woman's Club Salon." My former teacher Frances Greenman exhibited a flower piece, and other well-known Minnesota painters like Dewey Albinson, Lowell Bobleter, and Elof Wedin were also included. I finally got to show with some of the big names who had been big shots when I was a student in Minneapolis. I finally caught up to those guys. "George Morrison's self-portrait," wrote Sherman, "holds you by an introspective power dramatically realized in form and pigment."

I also wanted to join some exhibits of work by Native Americans, so I applied to the Philbrook Art Center in Tulsa, Oklahoma. But I was rejected. My art was too extreme; it wasn't Indian enough for them.

I never played the role of being an Indian artist. I always just stated the fact that I was a painter, and I happened to be Indian. I wasn't exploiting the idea of being Indian at all, or using Indian themes. But as my work became better known, some critics would pick up on my Indian background, and they'd make something of it. I guess they were looking for a way to understand my work.

That summer of 1946, I was back in Provincetown. We got free fish from the fishermen. One day, I put these mackerel on the table in our apartment. You know how fish can be just casually there, and they might affect you one way or another before you cook them and eat them. That's how I remember doing a series of paintings and drawings of fish. I began with the fish on the table, but then the fish forgot themselves and came to symbolize two people.

My paintings and drawings from Provincetown all show the beginning of a horizon line and above that, the clouds. The fish paintings had elements of

Untitled (Fish), 1945
Pen and ink, watercolor, and pencil on paper
9⅞ x 12⅞
Collection Minnesota Historical Society

Surrealism because the space was not realistic. The land was there, the water was there, then an arbitrary space projected the fish. The fish were large, superimposed against the background, which had the somber palette I used during this period. In works with two fish, I saw them again as symbolizing my relationship to Cicely. It was a sad story, both then and when her former boyfriend came back. The war had twisted him around and, after he married Cicely and their son was born, he ended up in a psychiatric ward. A very sad story.

The horizon line—I've done some paintings with low horizons, halfway down the canvas; and some even lower. But the ones from the later years on the lake have the horizon a quarter of the way from the top. In the earlier works I was trying for a vast horizon. That was my intention, to create a landscape behind the fish, reminiscent of the panorama of the bay. It was all imagined, though; I wasn't painting right from the landscape before me. I put it together in my head.

In the evenings, after going about their business being part of the summer art colony, old people, young people, mixtures of people frequented the bars in Provincetown where there was dancing and beer drinking. We young kids did a lot of so-called playing around; we used to close the bars every night.

I met my first wife, Ada Reed, that way. Like a lot of art students, she had the romantic idea of vacationing and painting in Provincetown. She went to a school there run by Henry Hensche, who was a *plein air* painter and also did portraits. His work was almost slick, but he had a way with color. He used to give demonstrations, maybe as far away as Cleveland where Ada was going to the Cleveland School of Art and living with her aunt. She spent the summers of 1945, '46, and '47 in Provincetown at the Hensche school.

She worked in a restaurant, too, as a waitress. I was drawn to her because she was an art student and she was attractive. The relationship with Cicely had been frustrating because of her friend coming back from Europe in 1946. Then I met Ada, mingling in bars, or going to the beach with a lot of kids. I never did eat at the restaurant where she worked—it was too expensive.

That summer the *Duluth News-Tribune* did a feature article on me and announced I was planning my first one-man show at the Hugo Gallery in New York. "The direction of his work, Morrison explains, is away from the literal, the maudlin and the narrative; toward the formal, expressive and lyrical." I might have said that; I don't know. The show at the Hugo Gallery never materialized.

December 1946 brought the Critics' Show at Grand Central Art Galleries in New York, a kind of gimmick to survey work done in New York at the time. Critics at New York magazines and newspapers each invited three younger artists to submit work. I was chosen by Ben Wolf, writer and editor for *Art Digest,* an art journal that doesn't exist anymore.

Wolf had frequented the Pyramid Group shows as a free-lance writer. A suave kind of guy, cosmopolitan, possibly with money in his family, he didn't seem to have to struggle to make a living. He liked writing reviews, a way of establishing himself as a critic.

My painting *Still Life* from 1944 won fourth place and $100. The *New York Times* called it, "powerfully organized . . . in somewhat the Cézanne tradition." I was happy to get all the notice, and the gallery bought the painting.

Grand Central Art Galleries was an academic gallery on the sixth floor of Grand Central Station, with a street address of 15 Vanderbilt Avenue. Not a well-known gallery, kind of middle-of-the-road. Though they were beginning to admit more liberal, so-called modern artists, they still had a lot of bad art—sugary, realistic, sentimental.

The Critics' Show helped me become better known. In the summer of 1947 I was asked to teach in Rockport, Massachusetts, at the Cape Ann Art School. William McNulty, a former League instructor, had started the school with his wife, a student of Morris Kantor. She was one of the many liberal students at the League. Rockport was a tourist town thirty miles from Boston on the tip of Cape Ann. Nearby was the fishing village of Gloucester. The whole area felt a bit like Provincetown. The McNultys' school was held above an old store on the main street in Rockport.

While I taught there, I entered a painting, *Subjugation,* in the Rockport Art Association's summer show that received a review in the *Boston Herald.*

After my first summer at Cape Ann, the McNultys gave up the school. So my friend Albert Kresch and I (both veering toward abstraction) took over the school and renamed it the Rockport Art School. We put ads in art magazines like *Art Digest, American Artist,* and *Art News,* and created a catalog with a quote from Ben Wolf on the back: "Through his semi-abstract idiom, this young and talented artist sings tellingly of . . . 'the rock whence he was hewn.'"

I mailed catalogs from my new apartment on 15 Leroy Street in Greenwich Village, where I'd moved to find lower rent and a place by myself. This place cost only $17 a month, a cold-water flat one stoop up from the street. Leroy Street was very close to Carl Ashby's frame shop on Cornelia Street, where I still worked.

My students at Rockport included Beverly Roman, a commercial artist also interested in fine art. She and her husband, Alex, started a big studio called the Litho Studio to produce pamphlets; she did the artwork, he the selling. It was very successful. She continued as one of my private students later in New York when I set up classes in my studio. She and her husband were among the first to buy a number of my works. Not at tremendous prices but enough to be satisfying to me.

The Rockport school lasted through the summer of 1948 under our direction, then it petered out. Al and I just about broke even.

I also acquired a poodle, Kobi, the result of a trade—watercolor for dog. Kobi came from a champion father bred in well-known kennels north of Boston, and his mother belonged to a well-to-do woman from Rockport. I named him after Kaaba, the holiest place of Islam, in Mecca, where Muhammad taught and where a coal-black meteorite had been housed since ancient times. I thought of Kobi's black coat and then of the meteor.

I had always wanted a dog because of growing up with dogs in Chippewa City. But they never were allowed in the house—never, never. Unheard of thing for a dog to come in the house. It was a different situation to own a good breed of dog instead of a mongrel like we had always had around the house.

George, Ada, and Kobi at Provincetown, ca. 1950.

Courtesy of George Morrison

When I returned to Provincetown after the two summers at Rockport, Kobi rode in the baggage car of the train, or traveled by car if I got rides with different people. So I managed to cope with the dog and the problems of the dog.

In 1947 my work went up in the Whitney's Annual Exhibition of Contemporary American Painting, at the Riverside Museum with the Pyramid Group, and at Grand Central Art Galleries. Around this time Grand Central created a modern art department called Grand Central Moderns and opened a second gallery at 55 East 57th Street. This second gallery was for the "finest progressive paintings and sculpture by young artists," so one of their their ads said. It was in the heart of the prestigious uptown gallery area.

Curators from all over the country came to New York to scout these galleries. They liked Grand Central Art Galleries and Grand Central Moderns because they were "in-between" galleries, showing neither all scenic work nor all abstractions.

I also began to be asked to send work all around the country—to Southern Illinois University, to New Orleans. My *Dream of Calamity,* a response to the bombing of Hiroshima and Nagasaki, was shown at the First Biennial Exhibition at the Walker Art Center in Minneapolis.

My definition of abstraction: no longer recognizable; completely devoid of any kind of reference to realism or naturalism.

In the trend of the times, people were going away from figurative work and toward so-called Abstract Expressionism. I happened to be in New York at a good time. The trend helped veer my own imagery toward abstraction.

Other things also had shifted. Take the motion picture and radio. They were part of a new immediacy in life, from telephone and telegraph and telecommunications to the motion picture. More immediate, more instant.

With abstract art the impact was immediate, too. You didn't have to look for a story in the picture. You could look at an abstraction and have an

Dream of Calamity, 1945
Ink and watercolor on paper
5⅞ x 9
Collection Tweed Museum of Art,
University of Minnesota, Duluth

immediate reaction. Then you might forget about it, or think about it. It lacked the sentiment of storytelling.

In my "Mystery Still Life" from 1942—I call it "mystery" because I can't remember where or when I painted it, though I would guess in Frances Greenman's class—even here, abstraction was coming into my painting. The objects are not clearly defined—one could be a vase, another a horn, another a cup or ashtray. The forms are suggestive.

Also, there are interesting accidental marks in the still life that are very appealing to me as a painter. When I go to museums, I look closely at the way artists put marks on the canvas. This goes for Rembrandt and for contemporaries like Mark Tobey or Cy Twombly. In a Rembrandt portrait, for instance, the thumb is very realistic, but it's done with one stroke of the brush. Like a magic thing. You look at it from a distance and it looks real. Then you look at it closer, and you can almost see the width of the brushstroke.

In my "Mystery Still Life," I let marks from the grain of the wood panel show through the paint. These marks—along with accidental marks of paint, strokes, variations in tone created in part by the direction of the strokes and whether they coincide with the grain of the wood—help make the painting what it is.

My work was going toward abstraction but I didn't jump into it. I was subconsciously feeling my way along. By this time all my paintings were studio

"Mystery Still Life"
("The Mystery"), ca. 1942
Oil on board
9 x 14
Collection of the artist

Untitled (Pink, black, gray), 1950
Ink and paint on paper
8½ x 11½
Collection Tweed Museum of Art,
University of Minnesota, Duluth
Gift of the artist

paintings, painted inside. All imaginative. I still began with subject matter—a whale vertebra, a piece of driftwood—then I built the composition around these.

I became preoccupied with texture. Scumbling, for instance. Scumbling is a technical term for laying the paint on with a palette knife and brushing it so that a bottom layer already on the canvas shows through. This creates texture.

I like the so-called magical surface of a painting, the marks a painter makes. This is different from the realistic portrait painters I had in school.

They knew exactly how to make flesh color, what paints to use. But when you get into imaginative painting, you let your subconscious suggest.

Now I was also coming around to the idea of making all kinds of scribbles on the canvas. Or putting a bright color here, a big area, then another color beside it. Making arbitrary shapes that didn't relate to anything like clouds or boats or the horizon line, just plain arbitrary shapes that were all over the canvas.

I could never have done this kind of abstraction in Minneapolis. Never, never, never. These influences were coming directly from Europe, through Kantor. Figurative elements in my work were becoming more obscure. Finally, I abandoned them and my work became totally abstract.

In New York, the melting pot, people didn't know what I was. They thought I was Persian because I was sporting a mustache. Maybe they thought I was a Persian businessman.

I kidded about it. It didn't bother me. I only thought about it later.

A lot of New York's multiracial people were prejudiced—like the "town Indians" who lived nearer to Grand Marais, often intermarried with whites, and looked down on the darker Indians in Chippewa City. By leaving for New York, I was freed from that discrimination at home, absolutely. But I found there was prejudice in New York, too, alongside acceptance in the big city.

Then in Provincetown, I met what they call Black Portuguese from the Azores. A lot of these people were very dark, many from North Africa, intermingled with people from Portugal and Spain. I think I got along with them maybe because of being close in color. Actually, we art students all got along with the Portuguese fishermen, became good pals, especially when we drank in the bars. But the lighter-skinned merchants in town were a little stand-offish, maybe against their own Portuguese relatives, maybe against working-class Portuguese.

After summers in Provincetown, Ada came to New York to study. She and her roommate were trying to make it as artists in the big city. I saw Ada in New York and the romance began to build to a point approaching marriage.

I always see my background as different from any who are non-Indian. Ada came from a family of so-called educated people. White, very respectable, middle-class people from Detroit. Very square, very conventional, certainly not art-oriented.

My family was not educated. My mother never went to school, didn't learn how to write. My father went only to the fifth grade, but he knew how to write and how to translate in Chippewa. He had that bilingual knowledge. That was good, but it was absolutely different from Ada's father, who was an engineer.

Our wedding in 1948 wasn't fancy—not a wedding where families were involved, just a wedding in a city hall. Some cousins came, maybe her family, but it wasn't a big deal. Shortly after, we went to visit her family in Detroit. I suppose they accepted me because I was married to their daughter. I got along with them, and I think they got along with me all right.

My family never met Ada's family. The possibility wouldn't have come around—her family wasn't coming to Duluth, and my mother wasn't going to Detroit. I don't think they would have fit together very well.

In 1948 I had my first one-man show at Grand Central Moderns. The show opened April 27 with a preview reception and was announced with a red and black brochure. Eighteen medium-sized paintings hung on the walls: *Driftwood, Shell and Bones, Plant Life, Organic Composition, Fish, Juxtaposition, Still Life, Whale Bone, Nightmare, Low Tide, Dream of Calamity, Bone, Confirmation, Dancers, Shell and Starfish, Pilgrimage, Subjugation, Self-Portrait with Sophisticated Girl.*

Grand Central Moderns was like all the other galleries on 57th Street. The buildings had probably been stores at one time, then were converted to galleries. The walls were painted off-white, pretty standard for galleries, and the floors sanded and polished. At the reception, mixed drinks were customarily served and simple hors d'oeuvres. The openings were always sociable affairs.

I was still pretty shy, but the broadening association with the world at large and my friends from art school helped me over it.

Some of the best breaks come through personal connections. You know a gallery director, or a friend of a gallery director, or an artist friend who will recommend you highly. Then a show is arranged. That's how this first show came about. Harold Jackson, manager of the Grand Central Art Galleries modern art department, saw a series of my paintings and liked my work.

Perhaps the most interesting review I got was written by Helen Carlson for the *New York Sun.* "Unconsciously or otherwise, these figures and forms derive from the ideography of Morrison's forebears," she wrote. "Even the crude, compelling harmonies of earth tones, smoldering reds, empyreal blues and molten oranges might have been fired to the canvases centuries ago in the primitive kilns of his ancestors." Critics will refer to my Indian background to try to make sense of the work. I wasn't pushing it, but they found it anyway.

George (right) with Harold Jackson, manager of the Department of Modern Art for Grand Central Art Galleries, at George's first solo exhibition in New York, 1948. Between them is *Driftwood* (1947).

Morrison scrapbook

It was a surprise to be reviewed by a newspaper from Basel, Switzerland, the *National-Zeitung.* Their reviewer didn't evaluate me as an Indian artist but saw me "as one of the many artists who seek an expression of their own within the meltingpot [*sic*] of America." She pointed out my "tendency to dramatize castaway symbols of civilization . . . : spooky treetrunks [*sic*], shells, bones, dead fish, and whale skeletons." She means the found wood and found objects from my beachcombing. Her review was a good one and helped me get a Fulbright Scholarship to France later on.

The year of my one-man show, IBM bought my painting, *Starfish.* The starfish has the quality of dancing figures from my earlier work. IBM bought it right out of the show. It was an honor; they had a tremendous collection and their own gallery on 56th Street. They were one of the first major corporations to acquire works by artists at different levels. My painting was small, and I wouldn't be surprised if it cost under $200.

When we were first married, Ada, Kobi, and I lived in my old Greenwich Village apartment. A very small, very cheap apartment on Leroy Street, pretty much in the heart of the Village. No central heat; our apartment had to be

Untitled (Green and brown whorls), 1949
Ink and watercolor on paper
11¾ x 9
Collection Minnesota Museum of American Art
Gift of the artist

Fallen Tree, 1950
Gouache [on unknown support]
18 x 26
Location unknown
Photo courtesy of George Morrison

heated with a stove. It served me well for three or four years. Then Ada and I shared it for a couple of years.

Ada had a flair for color; she did batiks. I still have an unfinished batik of hers. It was beginning to be a landscape, reminiscent of the rooftops near our place. Her batik, printed as is usual on silk, had certain, almost abstract qualities that were fitting into my head at that time, too. That's probably why I got it. She also sold a number of batiks, very colorful, attractive.

During this time I did a number of works in ink and watercolor or tempera. The color was laid down first, painted thin in places. Some of the open areas were just the paper or thin layers of paint, with crosshatching of texture over that.

Compare these works with *Fallen Tree* from 1950. Up in the sky lots of shapes, organic shapes. Very sculptural. The background is almost arbitrary, dark and light. It could be water, it could be land. The only sure thing is that this is a landscape, and the log is there. I intended the log as a personage, that's its symbolism. But you can also relate to its tactile quality. And its ambiguity—the log might be on the shore; it might be in the water.

Sometimes the effect of Expressionism is to transform the expected. For example, I don't draw clouds in a pretty way, blue and white, associating them with pretty clouds you've seen. Instead, I give the clouds a rugged shape, as in *Fallen Tree,* shape them like fish. And the tree is barely a tree anymore, just a suggestion of it.

The painting is gouache, a waterbase paint, that allows for quicker drawing than oil. I used a lot of whites, a lot of scumbling.

In November of 1949, my father died at the Cloquet hospital. I knew he was sick. Then my brother wrote that he died. I came right away to be with the family for the funeral. My mother had already separated from him and was living in Duluth. My father, Jim, and his close brother, Joe, had been sharing our old home there in Chippewa City.

The funeral was pretty much like funerals that I remember in Chippewa City. The casket was in the center aisle of the church, placed on sawhorses. I don't remember if a priest was there or not because it was winter. They prayed in Indian and then the pallbearers took the coffin out, put it in a hearse, and drove to the graveyard. Then there were more prayers as they lowered the coffin.

I didn't mourn my father in any conventional way. I felt respect for the family, the closeness of father-son-family. I knew that my father loved us in his own way, but he was more attached to us as infants; then as we grew older, he grew apart. He was not a mean man, not violent. He was an alcoholic and, I suppose, abusive with words in some ways. That was his manner.

Two or three months later, his brother Joe died. It seemed like he wanted to die.

Earlier that year I had been in Minnesota for two shows of my work—one at the Hart Art Gallery, run by Mr. and Mrs. Avon Hart in Duluth, and following that, a show at the Douglas County Historical Society in Superior,

Wisconsin. The *Duluth Herald* identified me as a Chippewa Indian who had lived in Grand Marais and Duluth, and mentioned my East Coast shows, calling me "uncompromisingly modern" and my work "complex and sophisticated." It is interesting that crafts by "Chippewa artists of the Nett Lake reservation" were shown with my work.

When I was home for my father's funeral in December, that same newspaper writer, Earl Finberg, interviewed me. I sounded very serious about New York, which I guess was true at the time. Along with the article was a photo of my painting *Starfish* that had been bought by IBM. I was certainly proud of that.

The year 1950 was a busy one, with my second one-man show at Grand Central Moderns and many group shows. The one-man show was held in May at the gallery's downtown address in the train station. I exhibited all new work, almost all landscapes or cityscapes or abstractions.

One review noted that my work contained what it called the "decorative genius in American Indian culture. . . . Whether the themes are pure abstracts, . . . or closer to the conformations of a landscape, Morrison approaches them primarily as a color patternist." That's an interesting phrase, "color patternist." I suppose it fits.

The next two years brought me many more group shows—the Walker biennial in Minneapolis and shows at the University of Nebraska, the Toledo Museum of Art, and the Brooklyn Museum. I also showed a couple of times with the group of artists at the Tanager Gallery in the East Village. The Tanager group was much like the Pyramid Group, and occasionally they asked others from the outside to join them in a show.

In 1951 *Confirmation,* a painting from my days at the Art Students League, was exhibited in Tokyo at the Third Tokyo Independent Art Exhibition. I was happy to see it turned into a postcard with the title and my name in Japanese.

I've often analyzed paintings according to the way I walk. My left leg is shorter and I walk at an angle. In my paintings, there's always a little leaning off center, obliquely to the right. I see this as some of the subconscious coming out—you don't know how or why.

PASSAGE: FIRE RIDGE

By 1952 Ada and I had moved out of our one-stoop-up apartment on Leroy Street into a much bigger loft on 23rd Street. The loft owners were going to fix it up pretty nice, but before they could do that, I heard I had received a Fulbright Scholarship to France.

From home, the *Cook County News-Herald* announced my scholarship: "Chippewa City to Paris—that's the stride that George Morrison, local artist, has achieved." The *Duluth News-Tribune* picked up the story and printed my painting *Structural Landscape,* calling it "one of the paintings which won" me the scholarship.

It was also a big deal in New York at the time. Students from various parts of the United States were converging on New York, getting on the *Queen Mary,* and going to Europe.

That September day we sailed, friends saw us off on the boat; they came with gifts and champagne and made a party. Sailing on the *Queen Mary* definitely was a highlight for all of us, including Kobi. At first we weren't sure we could take him. But then we arranged for him to travel on the first-class deck where all the animals were kept. I waved good-bye to New York from first class, before bedding down Kobi for the night and returning to my own third-class accommodations.

1952-1954

Fulbright Scholarship

Life in Paris

Move to Antibes

Work and shows
in France

Whitney Fellowship

Move to Minnesota

Return to New York

Divorce

Structural Landscape (Highway),
1952
Oil on canvas
22⅝ x 49½
Collection Joslyn Art Museum,
Omaha, Nebraska

Ada and Kobi and I stayed three months in Paris at the start. We found a two-room apartment near the Courbevoie bridge, near La Grande Jatte. Courbevoie was on the outskirts of Paris. La Grande Jatte used to be a park back in the days of Seurat, when he painted his famous *Sunday Afternoon on the Island of La Grande Jatte.* When we were there, the park was changing into an industrial area.

Our apartment was fairly pleasant, airy and sunny and near the Seine. We

took a train to the main part of Paris, near the Cathedral of Notre-Dame, and the areas of the Latin Quarter near the Church of Saint-Germain-des-Prés, and up in the hills of Montmartre where a lot of artists hung out. We'd partake in the Paris activities of students, going to museums like the Louvre, and looking into galleries and book stalls.

I enrolled at the Ecole des Beaux-Arts. It was part of the arrangement for Fulbright students. A lot of the Fulbright kids that year lived in Paris. Paris at the turn of the century had been the capital of the art world, and it was still full of artists and galleries. It would have been a great experience to stay longer. I might have learned the language better and met more artists. As it was, I did make some connections for shows with some Americans in Paris.

Then I had a chance to get a villa down in Antibes, so we went south with Dan Snyder, another Fulbright painter, and his wife. We got the villa for 25,000 francs for six months, which was relatively cheap at the time. To establish my student status, I enrolled at the University of Aix-Marseilles in Aix-en-Provence.

When we had first arrived in Paris in September, the weather was fine, sunny and pleasant. By the time we left for Antibes in December, approaching Christmas, it was getting cold. Even so, as soon as we arrived at the villa, I went swimming in the sea. It was cold, as cold as the lake at home.

The villa had *chauffage central,* central heating, but we couldn't afford to heat the whole house. So we spent most of our time in the big central kitchen with its cooking stove. We each had separate bedrooms that were cooler.

Regrettably, we couldn't afford to eat out, so our experience with French food was limited. We did most of our own cooking, picking up simple things like French breads. Our salads were probably pretty much American. The markets were very handy and cheap. We ate *poitrine,* chest meat, or short ribs. Good to make stews or other dishes.

In Europe I did a lot of things on paper, some with wash and ink, some gouache; very few oils because of the bulk, the handling and carrying. I was still playing around with abstract ideas, starting with automatic drawing, covering the surface with different kinds of texture. The work starts out that way, but it's more formal in the end. Not haphazard; it's all organized, connected up, making little cubistic sections.

I did a lot of drawing in the big room and sometimes in our bedroom. Then when it was sunny, I went outside to the big backyard, with many eucalyptus trees. Our villa was right on the Mediterranean, half a block from the water. You could see the Alps in the distance.

This area of the coast is called the Côte d'Azur, a fancy name for the French Riviera, another fancy name. It was very attractive to tourists. A lot of English people and French from other parts of the country congregated there.

We didn't do much traveling while we were on the French Riviera; we didn't have a car. But we did see Cézanne country around Aix-en-Provence. And we went swimming near Picasso's studio. We were familiar with all the little towns along there.

Not much traveling until the end of our sojourn in Antibes, when we went to Italy and Spain. When we left the villa in May—the rent went up for the tourist season and we couldn't afford it—we took Kobi with us. Italian train travel was hard, standing up and then worrying about the poodle in the baggage car.

Kobi always attracted attention. Especially at first when he was fancy clipped, he was very elegant. I remember, especially in Naples in the poorer sections, people stopping to look at him. Then he got more shaggy, more acceptable as a common dog.

In Spain we went to the island of Majorca with some friends. We had met them on a beach in France. Then they went to Spain and invited us to visit them for a month.

Meanwhile, back in Paris that spring, my work was part of a show at Galerie Craven, 5 rue des Beaux-Arts. I showed *Rooftops,* kind of a pastelish work I'd done in New York, bland, the paint was not very thick. This show of American painters was essentially put together by several of the painters after an arrangement with another gallery fell through. It included some names that are still well known, like Sam Francis and Claire Falkenstein. And some friends of mine like Arthur Deshaies, a radical painter I had met in Paris, a good friend who married a Fulbright pal of mine, Ruth Dryden.

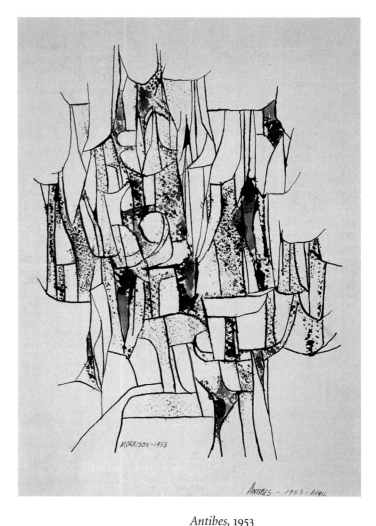

Antibes, 1953
Ink on paper
11 x 8½
Collection Minnesota Historical Society

Two newspapers reviewed the show and mentioned my work. *Combat: Le journal de Paris* was a leftist paper, more radical; maybe that's why they elected to write about me. *Arts Spectacles* also wrote a few lines about my painting.

In July at the Galerie Jeanne Bucher, on the Boulevard du Montparnasse—a good address on the Left Bank—another group show of Americans in Paris was held. Colette Roberts, the director of Grand Central Moderns in New York, was French herself; she set up this exchange of American and French artists. We Americans were selected from the Critics' Show of 1946 to exhibit in Paris. Then in October a group of Parisians from the Galerie Jeanne Bucher were exhibited in New York.

This time my painting *Pacific* drew some unusual description from *Les arts* and *Combat*. The French writer said my painting reminded him of Mexican painters. He insisted that I felt Indian and that my "whole work stands out as a quest for the traditional esthetics of [my] race." He used my ability to show in various museums as evidence that "when willing, North America can forget racial and traditional bondage." And *Combat* scolded the American colonists for wishing "to destroy a people . . . who possessed a flawless system of their own." That writer, Louis-Paul Favre, found that my work heralded "the resurrection of an entire race . . . almost wholly exterminated."

These reviews sound intelligent, but they were trying to be politically correct, making a big deal out of my Indian background.

While I was still in Europe, I heard that I received an Opportunity Fellowship from the John Hay Whitney Foundation. It would have been good to use that fellowship and stay in Europe. But Ada and I had started to separate. She wanted a family and I wasn't for it, at that time anyway.

In the fall of 1953, we came home and moved to Duluth, renting a house on the West Tischer Road in the Homecroft area. Maybe I wanted to be back in Minnesota or back with my family, I'm not exactly sure. With the fellowship, I had money to live on without having to work.

An article about us, with a lot of pictures, appeared in the *Duluth News-Tribune* in February 1954. One photo showed my painting *Construction* that had

George in Duluth, 1954. On the wall (clockwise from top left) are his paintings *Whalebone* (1947), *Confirmation* (1945), and *Driftwood* (1947).

Duluth News-Tribune (Earl Johnson)

recently been purchased by the Walker Art Center out of its fourth biennial show of Midwest artists. Ada was planning to write "an illustrated children's book that stars Kobi," our poodle, said the article. I don't think she ever wrote it.

There wasn't really much going on in Duluth. I got a small class of adults together every Thursday in the Arnold School nearby. And I painted.

By this time I was working almost entirely as a studio artist, working from imagination so I didn't need the real atmosphere around me. I was back in my own country, near my people, particularly my mother in Duluth. I worked primarily at night in imaginative ways. I also met some people who had a little photography shop and an interest in art. They put on a few shows.

During this period a few of my works were exhibited in a show of Native American artists sponsored by the Department of the Interior and the Indian Defense Association of Northern California. The show was hung in the M. H. de Young Memorial Museum in Golden Gate Park, San Francisco.

I guess my work stood out. I was not painting what the *San Francisco Chronicle* reviewer Alfred Frankenstein called neat, decorative illustrations of Indian dances, games, and other ceremonies. "Only rarely, as in the case of paintings by Oscar Howe, does one find anything in this style which has power of eloquence of design." I don't know if I agree with that, though I like Oscar Howe's work. But maybe Frankenstein was right to blame white schoolteachers for pressuring Native artists into an illustrating style. I don't know. I'm glad he liked my work; I was one of the few who he said "are sufficiently creative to go back to primitive Indian forms and develop them in their own ways."

I also met some Native artists in New York. Yeffe Kimball, an Osage from Oklahoma, for example, was easy to meet because she was an aggressive kind of person and she championed Indian rights relating to the arts. She was instrumental in getting shows together at the Philbrook and showing Indian art as a whole. She was doing this in the '50s, even before the civil rights movement stirred people up. She made people aware. Her art, like that of a lot of artists, was going through a progression, relating first to tribal art, then moving towards the trends of the day, toward abstraction.

I didn't start showing at the Philbrook's annual Indian shows until the early '80s. Earlier, they were strict about what they let in. They wanted things related more to tribal art, Indian themes. Now it's pretty open. There's more understanding of the diverse kinds of art made by Native peoples.

By March of 1954 Ada and I were back in New York for a show of my paintings at Grand Central Moderns. The *New York Times* said the paintings symbolized nature in "flat, key-like patterns. . . . clean-cut and laid decoratively like the inlaid designs on a marble floor." It was good to be back in New York.

I realize now, though, that I may have made a mistake coming back from Europe. It would have been good to use the Whitney fellowship to stay there. But my marriage to Ada was ending. I took it kind of hard. After we separated, I never saw her again. Kobi, who was with me when Ada and I were married, became a companion after she and I divorced. Over the years I kept track of Ada through her cousin, a friend of mine. Ada remarried and had two children, one of whom died. I heard from her cousin that she became a tragic woman. I don't know if that is true, but that's what I heard.

DREAMS OF DESTINATION: EARTH SONGS

I met Jackson Pollock once at the Cedar bar in Greenwich Village—through Kobi. Pollock was attracted to the dog and began to ask questions. He may have had a poodle himself. I didn't quite know who he was, but he introduced himself, "I'm Jack Pollock."

By then he was well known as one of the so-called big boys who had started Abstract Expressionism. But he still liked to come around and be sociable, sit in a booth at the Cedar bar. He and Willem de Kooning and Franz Kline. They all came to the Cedar bar. The bar wasn't a showy place with artwork on the walls. It was just a common bar. Dark wood and booths. Bland would be a good word for it.

Though they were the "big boys," gestural painters at the height of their notoriety, the camaraderie was such that they didn't walk around and act superior. They were friendly to everyone. All, in their way, were hard drinkers, one of the characteristics of the group.

Kobi and I moved into a large loft on East Ninth Street near Cooper Union. We had the whole floor of a building that I converted into a huge studio. A smaller section was the living area. The loft was close to the Cedar bar and to the center of the Village. I was working again at Carl Ashby's frame shop and showing occasionally in the little galleries in the Village.

1954-1959

Meeting the "big boys" of Abtract Expressionism

Gestural paintings

Big and little shows

The New York scene

Honors in Grand Marais

Teaching in Minneapolis

By now, these shows contained the "big boys" as well as everyone else. A lot of people had one-man shows. They wanted to spread their thoughts and move up in the art world, to get in bigger collections, private collections as well as museums. So all this activity generated little galleries like the Tanager Gallery, the James Gallery, the Phoenix Gallery, the Nonagon gallery. These were really lofts in old buildings, emptied of all signs of the stores they had been, their walls knocked out to make gallery spaces big enough for the big works of these artists.

Some of these loft shows included such well knowns as Lee Bontecou (a woman), Willem de Kooning, Philip Guston, Hans Hofmann, Franz Kline, and many more of us less known, all showing together. The art crowd liked these shows, and a lot of non-art people came to be seen. It was like a game, being part of the art scene.

I belonged to a group called Audubon Artists. In 1955 they gave me a certificate of honorable mention for my painting *Structural Landscape.* It was nice to belong to some of these groups because they had annual shows. Like the Federation of Modern Painters and Sculptors. Before and just after the war, this was a fairly radical and socialist group.

Many artists had leftist leanings, including myself. It was not that we were card-carrying Communists or anything like that, but we would vote for someone on a liberal ticket.

Some of the Abstract Expressionists formed a club; they were writing a manifesto. I didn't get involved with that, probing into the act of creation. Some were outspoken in both writing and speaking. I think I was just one of many followers, part of the group.

At the Riverside Museum in 1955, the annual exhibition of the Federation of Modern Painters and Sculptors included people who were already well known or on their way: Josef Albers; Milton Avery; Will Barnet; Cameron Booth, who taught in Minnesota; Louise Bourgeois; Lyonel Feininger; Morris Kantor, my former teacher at the Art Students League; Louise Nevelson; and Vaclav Vytlacil, also a former teacher.

In 1956 I showed *Luminous Landscape* in the Whitney's annual show. This show traveled to a couple of cities where it was reviewed: Louisville, Kentucky, and Quincy, Illinois.

I got into larger-scale work in the middle '50s, following the Abstract Expressionist trend. Walter P. Chrysler Jr., a well-known collector, bought some of it. He inspired a lot of artists to work big—part of a general movement at the time to enlarge the scale, get more heroic, more important.

Everyone in New York knew Walter Chrysler. He liked to play around with collecting artists and collecting art. He also established an art museum at Provincetown that showed many local and New York artists. He was a friend of many artists and helped them by buying their paintings.

He bought three of my paintings at different times. *Aureate Vertical* was one. Like others at the time, it was probably a one-shot thing, painted in one take. I was beginning to pay attention to vertical forms, yet retaining a suggestion of a landscape. You could say paintings like *Aureate Vertical* had structures within a landscape space.

I also sometimes let go of space entirely. In these paintings there is no reference to a horizon line or anything; it's open space. That was typical of what some of the painters in New York called endless space. Where you go out beyond the canvas; the painting seems as if it could go on and on in all directions.

Though a few of my canvases around that period were this bigger scale, my work as a rule was smaller. I still did a lot of drawing. More intimate, sketchbook-size paper. I was on the move a lot; the smaller format was easier to carry with me.

I contend that even a small drawing can be an important work.

A lot of my work emerged out of scribbles, part of the automatic drawing technique that came to us by way of the French, the Dadaists. They, in turn, were influenced by the associative thinking deriving from psychoanalysis. Frottage, when you rub charcoal or a pencil over paper placed on a surface with a pattern, was also a technique used by the Dadaists.

Aureate Vertical, 1958
Oil on canvas
48 x 80
Collection The Chrysler Museum of Art,
Norfolk, Virginia
Gift of Walter P. Chrysler Jr.

I think of my scribbles that led to images as a combination of frottage and automatic drawing. In arbitrary patterns, you put shapes on the canvas and then you elaborate on them, put layers over them, or modify them as you go. Sometimes the paintings were one-shot things, done in one stretch.

Pollock's *The She-Wolf,* a transitional work between Surrealism and Abstract Expressionism, shows you the wolf through all kinds of markings that cover the image. That was right up my alley; I was in that realm myself. Formalizing images that came out of scribbles or masses of paint. That became a way of working for me—daubing areas of color, or making marks with scribbles. My works were not entirely all over the surface, but there was no recognizable subject matter either.

I went through a period of using thick paint, starting from the late '50s all through the '60s. This gave more immediacy to the painting. Putting the paint on without thinning it with oil, or using acrylic paint without any water added. Putting it thick on the brush and then on the canvas with broad strokes, showing the thickness and movement of the pigment. Some of the paints were right out of the tube, like cobalt blue and burnt sienna. Some were mixed, like lavender and light blue, but otherwise, the colors were raw.

Untitled, 1960. Detail.
Oil on linen
31½ x 76½
Collection Minneapolis Institute of Arts

This was my version of gestural painting, which the other Abstract Expressionists like Pollock and de Kooning were doing. This was typical of things going on in painting at the time—gestural immediacy. Movement of the paint became an integral part of the idea of painting. There might be a suggestion of subject matter, as in a landscape that I called *Pier* because it looked structural. But the phenomenon of paint was what the painting was really about. Rather than getting sentimentally involved with a subject, the artist was more conscious of the paint itself, and that became the painting.

My life was going up and down, but there was always a progression, a progression toward the good. I like to think I was going slowly up. The work always shifting and changing.

At that time I usually got a couple hundred dollars for a small painting. Maybe $400 for a larger one. Of course, a dollar was worth much more, but neither then nor later did I ever make enough from painting to live on. Selling here and there, I got enough from other jobs to be comfortable for an artist of my level.

There were little shows all the time in the East Village. In 1957, the James Gallery Invitational Annual. Some good names here, including mine—Elaine de Kooning, Willem de Kooning's wife; Ilya Bolotowsky; Norman Bluhm; Grace Hartigan; Joan Mitchell; Robert Motherwell; Mark Rothko. Or 1959, the Phoenix Invitational, in the gallery at 40 Third Avenue. I knew a lot of these artists. We were all thirty-five-ish, fortyish, including Peter Busa, who later taught at the University of Minnesota; Mark Sammenfeld, a New Yorker; and James Wiegand, a fairly well-known artist from Tennessee. He and Red Grooms had come to Provincetown, both talented. Red Grooms became very well known. Wiegand—I don't know what happened to him, he was a good painter. Maybe he taught somewhere.

In the winter of 1957, I had another one-man show at Grand Central Moderns, which had moved to 1018 Madison Avenue, still uptown. I knew the people who made the brochure for me, a four-fold design on bright fuschia paper. Then I used one of my black-and-white drawings to finish it off. This was my first one-man show since 1954. A lot of the titles of paintings were related to semiabstract ideas: *Borealis* after the Northern Lights; *Estival,* a kind of landscape; *Traversal,* another extension of the landscape idea. I was also still working with the rock and quarry themes that I had started at Rockport. *Stratae, Quarry, Paleoform*—these titles all related to geology.

Colette Roberts, the gallery director, noted in the press release that I had painted all but one of these within the last ten months before the show. "Unlike the 1954 exhibition . . . painted in relatively cold colors," she wrote "the general effect of the present show is that of glowing warmth. . . . Morrison applies to his wide variations of red the same restraint as is usual in his work [but] there is a well-controlled boldness in his new exhibition."

Several works from the show were purchased, including *Antagonist* by the Whitney and *Dawn* by the Memorial Art Gallery at the University of Rochester in New York.

In 1958 the town of Grand Marais honored me with a dinner and a special exhibit of my paintings. My mother came up from Duluth. She was

George's mother, Barbara, at an exhibit of his work in the 1950s. The painting shown, *Landscape* (1953), is now in the collection of the Minnesota Museum of American Art.

Courtesy of George Morrison

a supporter of my work; she didn't understand much about it, or the process of learning or being curious like artists are, but she supported it. Two of my brothers, Jim and Roger, and two sisters, Josephine and Myrtle, came, too. Grand Marais High School, where I had graduated, bought a painting that is hanging in their library. Kind of a big deal for a town honoring an artist.

I saved all the clippings from that show. Wilhelmus Bryan, director of the Minneapolis School of Art, where I had gone, was the main speaker, and the Cook County Historical Society presented me a Distinguished Citizen's Award for the centennial year. (Minnesota had become a state in 1858.) I was also happy to see Mrs. Hal Downey, a summer resident in Chippewa City who had encouraged me when I was in high school. When I was a student at the Minneapolis School of Art, I kept in touch with her. She and her husband bought a small work of mine, not a major painting.

At the dinner I spoke briefly and thanked my friends the Anderts and the Downeys. "They made me forget I was from the wrong side of the tracks," I was quoted as saying in the *Cook County News-Herald.* "Mrs. Downey gave me courage to go out and make something of myself."

Around the same time, the State of Minnesota presented me with the Order of the North Star, which was also a centennial recognition and a nice honor.

This visit gave me an opportunity to return to Minneapolis and talk to Wilhelmus Bryan about becoming a guest instructor at the Minneapolis School of Art. It worked out; I agreed to spend three months teaching there the following year.

New paintings that year I titled with things celestial: *Spectrum Auroris, Helio-stratic, Paracosmic.* These went into another one-man show at Grand Central Moderns in 1958. Colette Roberts noted that, whereas last year's work used "small geometrical patterns carefully delineated," this new work featured "a flowing symphony of colors, closely related or subtly complementary."

The "endless space" of Abstract Expressionist paintings—where the painting seems to go in all directions—struck some people as explosive and destructive. Destructive of the objective in painting, not showing a literal subject matter. But there was the cool, hard-edged, more geometric kind of abstraction, too. These various forms of abstraction were all going on at the same time.

In the mix of art and people that contributed to the camaraderie, drinking, and parties at Greenwich Village bars and clubs, there were a number of jazz musicians who were moving in new directions, too. I had gotten interested in jazz way back in the '40s, listening to Dixieland at little clubs. Then Charlie Parker and the introduction of bebop took the musical world by storm. It didn't seem to fit in logically—it wasn't coming out of Dixieland. I— and a lot of other people—thought it was extraordinary that Parker had this strange music coming out of him. Unique.

Bebop opened up a lot of things, like the so-called new sounds coming from Stan Getz, Dave Brubeck, and Gerry Mulligan in the early '50s. I went up to 52nd Street a couple of times to hear jazz musicians like Coleman Hawkins. But it was expensive to go to the uptown clubs—you had to pay a cover charge, whereas, at a bar like the Cedar, you could just buy a beer.

Near the Cedar was another one of my favorite places to go, a little jazz joint called the Five Spot. Thelonious Monk was starting to play there. That's where I heard him, and that's where I shook his hand one night.

It's the luck of being there at the right moment.

In February 1959 I taught at the Minneapolis School of Art. I liked the idea because it was near my former home and was my former school. The place had changed. Liberal factions had come in, freer toward the idea of abstraction.

While I was teaching there, the Kilbride-Bradley Art Gallery in Minneapolis gave me a one-man show of recent paintings. It was nice enough in its way, but I didn't like the headline the *Minneapolis Tribune* used: "Kilbride to Show Work of Indian Artist Morrison." Sometimes they tried to capitalize on that kind of thing.

Shortly after, when John Sherman reviewed the show, he didn't say anything about my being Indian. "[Morrison] has built up a national reputation," he wrote. "The paintings . . . strike inner chords while pleasing the eye."

The Kilbride-Bradley gallery featured me in their *Potboiler* broadside. There they mentioned museums that had purchased my work up to that point: the Walker Art Center, Minneapolis Institute of Arts, the Whitney, the Joslyn in Omaha, and other museums in Philadelphia, Atlanta, Richmond, Utica, and Rochester, New York. It was good to come back after fifteen years with so much to show, though I was far from well off.

After that brief stint in Minneapolis, I returned to New York. In December 1959, *Vogue* magazine featured twenty-three works of art for sale at New York galleries. "The artists stretch from living Americans to an unknown Greek sculptor who lived about 600 B.C.," said the blurb. "The price stretch: $36 to

$400." My painting *Quite Far* was listed at the top price range of $400. *Quite Far*—I was trying to get into more poetic, mysterious titles.

I had no trouble selling that piece.

My time at the Minneapolis School of Art was the beginning of getting a little teaching here and there. If your name was spread around and you were getting to be more known, then you were called upon to teach. A lot of artists in New York were doing that at the time. Some took jobs outside New York because the best jobs in the city were already filled by more established artists.

I began searching for more teaching, looking seriously at finding a more stable income than working at the frame shop or doing construction jobs.

PART TWO

In Part Two, George Morrison
is joined by his former wife
and fellow artist Hazel Belvo
in recounting their lives together.

CRIMSON RIDGE: PATH TO THE SKY

GEORGE: In the winter of 1960 I taught at the School of the Dayton Art Institute, replacing John King, head of the drawing and painting department, who was on sabbatical. This was my next success in locating teaching jobs after Minneapolis. You could say that Dayton got me going on teaching.

Dayton, Ohio, is an industrial town, mid-America. Related to the auto industry by way of tires and things like that. It was also near the Wright-Patterson Air Force Base. Dayton was about the size of St. Paul, as I remember it.

The Dayton Art Institute school was connected with the museum. The museum didn't have any spectacular art pieces, mostly older art and not of the best quality. My sense was that Dayton wasn't very progressive and stayed in its own way of thinking, but the director of the art institute, Tom Colt, and his wife, Priscilla, who was a good art historian, invited a lot of speakers from New York. Everyone who came to visit at the art institute was extreme like myself, and that included jazz artists like Gerry Mulligan, Bob Brookmeyer, and Zoot Sims. Not radical-radical, but they were involved with more advanced ideas. That's what Tom Colt encouraged. So when John King was going to leave, Tom Colt called up Yeffe Kimball in New York and asked her who he could invite who was new and interesting. She suggested me.

1960–1970

Teaching at the School of the Dayton Art Institute

Marriage to Hazel Belvo

Move back to New York

Son, Briand Mesaba Morrison, born

Hazel's account of their life and art

Rhode Island School of Design

Houses in Providence

Summers on the Cape

Beginning of wood collages

Untitled, 1960
Oil on linen
31½ x 76½

Collection Minneapolis Institute of Arts

Once I was there, the *Dayton Daily News* gave me an interview. They quoted me as saying, "Art is a changing thing . . . [we are] living in a fast age. . . . [T]he so-called realistic painting of today is a different art [than in the past], reflective of the abstract approach." You see, I was an abstract artist coming to teach in a place where many students were only beginning to get a glimpse of abstraction. The museum gave me a solo show in their Circulating Gallery and included my work in group shows with Dayton artists.

In the classroom I didn't twist anyone's arm to do abstract work. My teaching was pretty open. I often had a model available to give students a tangible reference. Or I would teach from a landscape, as I had in Rockport. Once students had an image, I taught them how to manipulate it. That was my way

of introducing them to the idea of abstraction. But I wasn't teaching abstraction, per se.

One of the paintings I did in Dayton was an urban landscape, *Untitled*, from 1960. It was a one-shot thing, the kind of thing I was trying to do at the time. *Mt. Maude* from 1942 was also done in one stretch—an afternoon on the side of the mountain. But the 1960 work was not determined by a condition of light or time of day, rather by the length of time I spent painting it— maybe six hours at night.

Here, I was trying to capture an inner thing. That was part of the Action Painting school, where you began with the act of painting itself, then images began to emerge. Almost like subconscious painting. The scale was becoming larger and the format more horizontal. There's an openness on the right. No indication of light coming from the outside, but the open part of the painting provides another way of defining space.

Again this could be related indirectly to *Mt. Maude.* There you get a clump of trees, like the dark part of the 1960 painting, and then you come out into an open field of light green grass, like the lighter corner of the later work.

John Weber bought the 1960 painting from me in my studio. He was a student out of Antioch College, in Ohio, who had begun working as an assistant curator at the Dayton Art Institute. I sold the painting to him for $200. John was a pretty close friend at the time. In later years he had a successful gallery in New York, which he still has. Eventually he gave the painting to the Minneapolis Institute of Arts.

At the Dayton art school I met a student named Hazel Belvo. She read about me in the Dayton paper and joined my painting class. The evening after the first class, I invited her to my studio.

HAZEL: We had a lot of speakers, musicians, and now a teacher from New York. I had learned a lot from my other teachers, but I was interested to hear

Hazel Belvo and George in 1966.

Courtesy of Hazel Belvo

George's new ideas. When I visited his studio after the first class, he was working on a large canvas, painting with pure pigment right out of the tube. It was a triptych done in what he called one-shot—that is, he stayed up all night to do the whole thing at once. It was a wonderful painting, raw and refined at the same time, a meeting of intellect and spirit. I felt as though we'd known each other forever.

GEORGE: Hazel was from a farming community near Dayton and was married, with two sons. She had done a nice portrait of her husband. When I first met her, she was a good portrait painter—that she had picked up from John King, the art teacher I was replacing. She handled paint well, but she wanted to veer away from the so-called academic style towards an Expressionistic rendition of her surroundings.

HAZEL: If I got a little experimental, John King used to say to me, "Now, Hazel, remember, you're a portrait painter." I learned so much from him, but George began encouraging me to be experimental. I did a portrait of George the first month I knew him, one of those images where I was trying to be experimental but didn't know how to be.

GEORGE: When I came along, she had been studying as a "student-at-large" for four years. Other influences had begun to creep in and she was experimenting with Expressionism and abstraction. Some of her first paintings in the new style were big, colorful, and flat in the Expressionistic sense.

Art opens your eyes to the world in many ways, broadens your mind. Her marriage was beginning to flounder. I guess she wanted to leave. I came along at the right time. We hit it off and I stayed in Dayton through the summer session. Then at the end of the summer, we decided to go to Provincetown.

HAZEL: George bought an old Dodge station wagon, a wonderful, sturdy old car with standard shift. I remember that the back did not close or lock. George packed a trunk of his art stuff. Then, since he had never driven, I did all the driving.

We drove to New York first. When we got there, we went directly to the Cedar bar. While I parked the car, George made a telephone call from a phone booth on the corner. He called Ruth Speaker, a friend of his, and asked if we could spend the night. Ruth said sure, come on up. We were going to have a few drinks first, he told her.

In the bar we sat down with two men and started talking. One turned out to be Franz Kline and the other Herman Cherry, a very good painter, though not with Kline's reputation. Soon, another guy came by and said hello; they called him "Bill." As we chatted, I realized that he was Willem de Kooning. I couldn't believe I was in the Cedar bar with all these stars, all friends of George's.

Finally George and I drove to Ruth's loft on 16th Street. I parked the station wagon, and we left the trunk in the back. It was four flights of stairs up to Ruth's, and George said he would come down later for the trunk. But as Ruth's door opened we were swept into a wild party. No one thought about the trunk until the next morning when George was walking Kobi. He looked into the station wagon and saw that the trunk was gone, stolen. George had traded drawings with Franz Kline, and the Kline drawing, which was worth a lot of money, was in the trunk. George lost his sketchbook, too.

Aside from that, seeing New York with George was wonderful. He introduced me to many artists who became friends. One of the great gifts George gave me was an introduction to Louise Nevelson, who showed with him at Grand Central Moderns. Louise became very important in my formative years. Finding a woman mentor back then was difficult, and Louise taught me a lot.

That first trip, George also showed me New York. I had been there before, but in those eight days George gave me a more complete understanding of the city—visually, as an island—than I had ever had before. We took the Circle Line tour around Manhattan. We went to a bar on a rooftop.

GEORGE: That was the Waldorf-Astoria.

HAZEL: We took the Staten Island Ferry.

GEORGE: Went to the Fulton Fish Market.

HAZEL: And to the famous Joy Garden Cantonese restaurant in Chinatown, where many artists gathered. Since then, I have used this same tour countless times to introduce my own students to New York.

GEORGE: As you can see, that was the beginning of our romance.

HAZEL: George formally asked me to be with him by saying, "How would you like to live in Minnesota?" Even then, he was interested in going back. My response was, "Does that include my children?" My two boys, Joe and Danny, were staying with their father on the farm.

GEORGE: We had been together for almost a year, getting to know each other in Dayton while we worked on our art, and I taught, met people, and had shows. Hazel's divorce had come through, and as we talked about getting married, we eventually decided on a date of December 13, 1960.

HAZEL: We wanted to have the chaplain at Antioch College marry us in the chapel, with our good friends John Weber and Laurie James as witnesses. When the day arrived, a raging storm came up and all the electricity went out. Under flickering candles, George and I became involved in working on a mosaic table he had started—a design in tile, broken china, and glass. The work was so compelling that we forgot the time. When the lights finally came on, we were shocked to find that it was 8:00 P.M., the hour the ceremony was supposed to start. And we still had to drive an hour and a half through the snow.

When we arrived, our friends John and Laurie had gone from being worried to being furious. But the champagne was chilling in the snow outside their house and the chaplain was still waiting.

GEORGE: We had talked about driving to Duluth after the wedding to introduce Hazel to my family.

HAZEL: But first we had a show together in our apartment on Forest Avenue.

GEORGE: This may have begun our habit of having studio shows together. They were kind of nice. They gave us a chance to get rid of some of our work at a lower price and make some money.

Later we continued to do this in our lofts in New York. We sent out invitations, typed and mimeographed, and usually got a good response. I knew some beginning collectors and other people interested in our work. They responded by buying something small.

HAZEL: Before we left for Duluth, I went to say good-bye to my mother. "You better take a pair of boots along," she said. "I understand it gets very cold in Minnesota." I borrowed a pair of her boots, the old zip-up kind with fleece lining. It was a good thing I did, because the heater in the Dodge didn't work and the front vents were rusted open.

We arrived in Duluth around midnight. I was frozen. George's mother and his brother Roger and sister Josie were waiting up for us. I was so numb I could hardly walk. After we were introduced, I asked George's mother if I could lie down. Always gracious to me, she showed me into the front bedroom. There was a curtain across the doorway; right outside was the phone.

As I was sitting on the bed taking off my boots, the telephone rang. "Oh yes, George is here," I heard her say. "Oh yes, brought his new wife with him. Oh yes, married another white woman."

GEORGE: That's a funny story about my mother.

HAZEL: When I heard that, I knew it was really significant, but I didn't understand how much. We both had a lot to learn. Expectations, communication styles—all were different. Later, some women in Grand Portage would help educate me about the differences. George would say to me, "That's Indian." The women would laugh and help me see what was cultural and what was Morrison. But for the moment, I was on my own. The women in George's family were always very loving and welcoming to me, but it took a long time for us all to be easy together.

GEORGE: On April 9, 1961, our son, Briand Mesaba—named after my mother's family—was born. We were able to sublet my former apartment at 216 East Sixth Street from the friend who had gotten it from me. Hazel's two other sons, Joe and Dan, stayed with their father, and she had the option of going back to see them or having them come to visit.

HAZEL: Franz Kline was Briand's godfather.

GEORGE: A godfather by our notions, not by any church notions. Franz elected himself Briand's godfather, as a nice gesture toward us, and we were happy about it.

HAZEL: We visited Kline's studio soon after Briand was born. As Briand lay on the big bed in Franz's room, everyone toasted him with champagne and called him "Mr. B." Above the bed hung one of George's paintings, a big red abstraction.

GEORGE: I had met Franz at the Cedar bar with many of the other artists. He was an open, curious-minded man, and he liked me partly because I was Indian and also a fairly good artist. We exchanged visits, and he came to like the red painting of mine. We decided to make a trade.

HAZEL: Franz took the red painting but he asked George to wait to choose one in return until after he had finished having a major show.

GEORGE: That was fine. While Franz had his show, we left the city for the summer in Provincetown. Unfortunately, while we were gone, Franz had a heart attack and died. The trade we had planned was never consummated. He had my painting. His ex-wife or girlfriend at the time couldn't care less about our arrangements.

"Red Painting" ("Franz Kline Painting"), ca. 1960
Oil on canvas
47 x 79
Collection Hazel Belvo

HAZEL: She was not willing to honor the trade or, for a while, give George back his painting, which Franz had hung in their Provincetown home. Eventually, with some finesse, George got it back.

GEORGE: Having a family prompted me to seek out more work. The summer of 1961 I taught at the Iowa State Teachers College in Cedar Falls.

The college bought one of my paintings, called *Crevasse,* and the head of the art department, Harry Guillaume, bought another. This was the period of my vertical paintings; they were horizontal in format, but the forms were vertical.

I also sold a painting to a couple who owned considerable farmland around the town; you could say they practically owned the town. These people were quite interested in the arts. They wanted to mingle with artists, which was good for a small town. The painting they bought had endless space.

Endless space was a term used by many Abstract Expressionists to define how their paintings seemed to go beyond the edges of the canvas. These artists flattened the space, too. Instead of the deep space created through perspective, which had been used in Western art since the Renaissance, the Abstract Expressionists flattened distance into a shallow space, pushing the distant forward, until all the action of a painting occurred on a shallow plane. Many of my paintings in this period had flattened space or endless space, however you look at it.

I also swapped paintings with Lester Johnson who taught at Yale for a long time. He had a painting of mine from this period called *Early Hours.*

Lester had gone to the Minneapolis School of Art but was kind of radical and eager to get out of there, so he hadn't graduated. He went on to the Art Institute of Chicago, then to New York. I caught up with him on the East Coast—a nice, bright—brilliant—interesting guy. I don't think he ever finished school anywhere, but he picked up what he needed from friends, more or less on his own. He just went further and further.

Now the big Lester Johnson painting I have is on Hazel's wall. He told me later that he had a fire in his studio and the painting of mine that I had given him went up in the fire. We never consummated any other kind of exchange.

HAZEL: In 1962 George taught at Cornell, in Ithaca, New York, for one semester and then at Pennsylvania State University for another. During this period Briand and I stayed in New York, in our loft on Avenue A and Sixth Street, where we moved after leaving George's earlier apartment. The loft was on the third story, and we became good friends with Newton and Helen Harrison, conceptual artists who lived below us. I was impressed with Newt; he was the first antiwar activist I had known, articulate and passionate.

In the afternoons, I would take Briand grocery shopping on Second Avenue. We could get what we needed for $5 a week because I shopped at the end of the day when fresh produce was marked down to a few pennies.

Hazel (left), holding Briand, and George (right) with Jack Wickline and Ruth Richards in a New York loft, ca. 1963.

Courtesy of Hazel Belvo

When we married, George had told me that he couldn't support me. Though it was terrible to hear in 1960 when you're pregnant, it was also freeing. It freed me to act on my own behalf, and on George's, too.

I was trained as a butcher. My mother had owned a wholesale packing company. She was a wonderful meatcutter, and from the time I was eleven until I was twenty-five, I had helped her. We dressed well and discussed cooking the meat with our customers. It was a custom business.

I had this skill but no way to use it—in New York, women were not allowed to join the union. So I made sculpture bases for the Museum of Modern Art for $1 each. Can you imagine?

After Cornell, George returned to doing carpentry work in New York. He has always crafted things beautifully. He and his friends were working on a loft for a wealthy couple, laying a teak floor.

With George doing carpentry and my small income, we had to find other ways of making a living. So we talked about possibilities. George had many options, as far as I could see, but he had never formalized his work history or business. I offered to do that for us, as a couple. I got his materials out of storage, sorted all the gallery announcements and brochures, and learned to create a professional resumé. George's resumé filled five pages. He had an impressive history.

GEORGE: It was Hazel who sent out over a hundred applications for teaching jobs.

HAZEL: Four responses came back. One was from Florida; neither of us wanted to go there. I liked Ohio State because we could be near my children. The third response I've forgotten, and the fourth was from the Rhode Island School of Design. George was disappointed that the University of Minnesota had not responded.

GEORGE: When I interviewed at the Rhode Island School of Design in Providence, they offered me an assistant professorship. I was happy to accept.

Being near Boston and the coast, Providence was a cultural center. Brown University was there, and the school of design. I think that helped create the town's liberal and progressive character. It had some New England character, too, the old Puritan ethic. But by and large it was progressive.

I started teaching in 1963 at the intermediate level, juniors and on up to graduate students. Dealing with liberal ideas. The school is known for that. This was more up my alley, though there were instructors who were more academic. One such colleague must have seen that the school was shifting to more liberal ideas because he retired soon after I arrived.

The school attracted students from all over. As always happens, a group of maybe thirty were outstanding. I became close friends with one, Alfred DeCredico. He always associated with the teachers because he was advanced—brilliant. He has been prolific in his abstract style of painting and very successful in getting shows. He now teaches at the school himself.

I assigned one book for beginners, more of a technical book on how to draw, with very liberal ideas. Occasionally, I also used my paintings as demonstrations. But that wasn't my usual way of working. Maybe I'd show them my sketchbook or draw something in my sketchbook as an example. That was one way of bringing across an idea.

Once or twice a week we would line up the students' paintings all around the room and talk about each one, exchanging ideas back and forth. They were learning from each other.

I think every instructor has something to say, and a student can learn from different people. Pick up an idea here or there and take it for what it is worth. Hopefully it's constructive. I learn from my students, too; that's one of the values of teaching—young people have lots of good ideas.

Then there were the student shows. I have always liked to organize student shows to give them a chance to compete. They see their work displayed in a professional way. It gives them a certain kind of pride, seeing their work outside the classroom.

I always thought that my teaching was more varied than academic instruction. Liberal persons like myself were beginning to take over, teaching academic painting as well as abstraction.

GEORGE: At first Hazel and I rented one of the oldest houses in Providence. We had met an eccentric millionaire who owned property all over town. He was a kind man; he took to us.

HAZEL: While his wife led Briand into the kitchen for cookies and milk, he said, "You want to live in my house, well, let's make a deal. How much money do you make? Then you should spend one-fourth to one-third for rent. That's how much I'll charge you." He called George "young fella."

GEORGE: The house was called Cole Farm; it was one of a group of houses on Cole Farm Court, built in the 1730s. The story goes that it was owned by a man named Brown, a person of means, later associated with Brown University. He eventually built himself a far grander house but during the Revolutionary War, Brown was still living in the farmhouse. In 1778, when General George Washington was in the area, he is said to have visited the house. How true that was, I don't know.

Cole Farm, named after the man to whom Brown sold it, was a typical New England house, with a slanted floor because it had settled on one side. We didn't mind. We fixed it up. That was one of the things in our verbal contract with the millionaire friend—he said we could do what we wanted. He supplied the materials, and we did some changing to suit our tastes. A garage connected to the house became a studio for Hazel and me. That was a good space. The house had gables and some rooms upstairs; a front porch overlooked a little lawn. The house was set on top of a knoll. Originally, a well had served as a water source.

HAZEL: We had a table in the kitchen where we all could fit. We often ate there, and afterwards George and I would play games with Briand. One of us would draw an apple with a bite taken out of it; then we'd draw another bite out, and we'd say, "How many bites are gone?"

George also made Briand a set of blocks that were really wonderful, out of 2 by 4's, 2 by 6's, and 2 by 8's. He shaped them into arches, rectangles, squares. The whole set was in Briand's room off the dining room.

Briand also played with Matchbox cars. When he'd let them go, they'd roll to the other end of the house. The floor slanted that much, thirteen inches from back to front.

One night George's friend from New York, Jim Rosenquist, came to dinner. Remember, this is the man who made all those big paintings on scaffolds.

GEORGE: He was a guest at the Rhode Island School of Design and stayed with us.

HAZEL: Dinner was ready after dark when Jim arrived. He brought a bottle of Jack Daniel's, and after dinner we had some drinks. Then he asked to go to the bathroom. When he got up, he didn't know what was wrong. He couldn't walk. It was the floor.

GEORGE: We stayed at Cole Farm for around three years.

HAZEL: Making all kinds of improvements. We took out walls, George built bookcases. I stripped wallpaper and painted everything. The bathroom was wonderful. I painted the claw-foot tub red, with a red ceiling and natural wood floor.

Sharing the studio in the garage was difficult because George fills his studios up, and I can't think unless the surfaces are clean. Still, we loved Cole Farm.

The "eccentric millionaire" who was renting to us visited me once a month to check on the house. He had become my friend, and he always brought me flowers. George and I laughed whenever he drove up in his old blue Chevy Impala—or rather when the uniformed chauffeur drove him up. The car was so incongruous.

After a while, I came up with the idea that we should buy the house. I asked him to sell it to us for $21,000, the price he had thought it was worth when we moved in. He agreed to do that. But when I asked him to put the agreement in writing, he insisted, "My word is my word. I never go back on my word." So I accepted his promise and we shook hands on the deal. Then Briand and George and I went to Provincetown for the summer.

While we were gone, our millionaire friend dropped dead of a heart attack. His sons and wife did not know or care about our agreement. They wanted to charge $37,000 for the house. It was very disappointing. We couldn't touch it at that price.

GEORGE: Our work life was more settled, but it was still a very social period. After I got the job at the Rhode Island School of Design, we used to go to New York for a couple of days to catch up on all our cronies and friends. Briand was three or four years old, and we'd have a babysitter take care of him.

HAZEL: I had kept our studio in New York. A friend rented it and let me come back for a week every month or so. The decision to move to Providence was hard for me; I had just been getting established in New York and, in many ways, had not wanted to leave.

GEORGE: I remember driving through Connecticut and sipping on vodka and orange juice. Then coming down the East Side Highway in Manhattan and feeling high already. That's risky, drinking while you're driving—that's dangerous. But it was part of the '60s for me, a destructive period. Jackson Pollock had been killed in a car crash in 1956—I don't know what the circumstances were.

During this period I was quite involved with drinking and playing around with various kinds of drinks. Gourmet cooking was connected to this, too. I remember one drink in particular—I called it a Surrealist drink. I mixed Italian bitters called Fernet-Branca with grenadine syrup and Guinness stout. Not a terribly strong drink but a good drink. I don't know if I was responsible for concocting it, but we had it on hand, and I began to associate it with myself. I used to serve it and drink it. I called it my drink.

Sometimes I think that being Indian and rather shy contributes to why Indians, including myself, like to drink. The minute we have a couple of drinks, we loosen up. My father was that way, too.

I was close to alcoholism growing up in Chippewa City. My father drank a lot. I don't think he was an alcoholic in the sense that he drank every day, but I guess he'd go on binges when he got some money. When we were kids in Chippewa City and Grand Marais, we took to drinking at a very early age. Some pals of mine and I used to buy big picnic bottles of wine, double liters. Like a lot of kids these days sniffing coke, wanting to get high.

GEORGE: We continued to spend summers on Cape Cod, in Provincetown, where we rented a small house right in town.

HAZEL: For me Provincetown became my family place. Good for the kids in the summer. For years I had all three of my sons with me every summer at 8 Law Street. It was my dream house, my home!

I had no trouble painting in Provincetown. I would put a sign on the door telling people not to bother me. I got a lot done. But for George, it wasn't so easy.

We first rented the lower floor at 8 Law Street with money from my fellowship from the Radcliffe Institute for Independent Study. Here all the kids could hang their swimming suits on nails and the next summer the suits would still be there when we came back. We rented the house from George

George, carrying Dan Belvo, and (from left) Hazel, Joe Belvo, and Briand Morrison at Longnook Beach, Truro, Mass., 1965.
Courtesy of Hazel Belvo

George and Hazel on Longnook
Road, Truro, Mass., 1965.

Courtesy of Hazel Belvo

Grotz, who wrote a book, *From Gunk to Glow,* on antiques. He and George were arch-enemies.

GEORGE: Not really. Good friends and arch-enemies. We played the thing up; we had a good time being enemies, drinking and arguing.

HAZEL: One time I was trying to make peace between them, and George Grotz said, "You're trying to destroy the only stable relationship I've ever had in my life, which is my dislike of George Morrison."

GEORGE: Hazel has always gotten a charge out of that story.

We spent a lot of time walking the beach. We found driftwood from all over the world—the South Seas, the Caribbean, the North Atlantic. It all washed up on this tip of Cape Cod. Some had bits of paint, half worn off. Some had rust stains or colors soaked in. Industrial boards were washed nice and gray. Nail holes added texture and color where rusted nails had oxidized the wood. There was an interesting history in those pieces—who had touched them, where they had come from.

I collected them and the kids collected them.

New England Landscape II, 1967
Wood construction
48 x 119⅞
Collection Amon Carter Museum,
Fort Worth, Texas

We crated some of the wood to ship back and brought some home in the station wagon. Boxes of choice pieces. I probably still have some.

With this wood, my work moved into a new form—large wood collages. From walking the beaches at Cape Ann and Provincetown, beachcombing on Martha's Vineyard and Nantucket.

HAZEL: I remember it was a big thing for the kids to know just the right piece to pick up, the "George" piece. George often said to the kids, "No, I can't use that one. It's got ragged edges." Everyone was invested in collecting the wood—that was one of the nice things about the collages.

GEORGE: I made my first large collage at Provincetown and exhibited it privately in the garage that I rented as a studio. The collage was big, constructed

on a background of plywood three feet by nine feet. I worked on a table about forty-two inches high, which I could walk around and sit next to on a stool. These collages were a good scale for me and lent themselves to large-scale exhibition. That encouraged me to step up collecting wood.

Soon I was making them in earnest. Luckily I had a big enough studio in Providence. The first collages I made, I was not successful in selling. But gradually, as I exhibited them, they picked up interest.

HAZEL: Some friends even sent you wood by mail or brought it back from other parts of the world to be part of a collage. If someone found a circle, it was very special. Interesting, distinctive pieces, like the top of an old scrub brush.

GEORGE: I still have that.

Paintings in wood—that's how I see them. They come out of my head. I make them from scratch, yet they are derived from nature, based on landscape. There's a horizon line in each one, about a quarter of the way from the top. That's an absolute straight line, made with a pencil, to help guide the work.

Before I made the first large one, I had played around with joining two pieces of wood together. I think my first one was made with wood that I'd picked off the streets of New York. Did I call it *Eighth Avenue Landscape*? Where the two pieces of wood met was the horizon.

In the large collages, the grain of the wood and the knots suggested the movement of clouds, sun, and wind. And below the horizon line, the rough water or beach. The gray, crusty, weather-beaten wood all added to the texture and suggestion.

I use the aesthetics of painting to guide my selection of wood for contrast and texture, color and shape. All this is formal, yet the driftwood itself gives a sense of history—wood that has had a connection to the earth, yet has come from the water. I realize now that in making these, I may have been inspired subconsciously by the rock formations of the North Shore.

GEORGE: When we had to leave Cole Farm, we bought two adjoining houses on Transit Street, in the older section of Providence near the waterfront—a section as old as the 1630s, when Roger Williams first founded the settlement.

As we started repairing and converting the house we lived in, we found under many additions a very fine nineteenth-century house; later we learned it had been built by Isaac Peck in 1825. We had known the approximate date when it was built—there were other houses even older in the neighborhood. People from the historical society were aware of the importance of the houses, and eventually the neighborhood was designated an historic district. The marker with the date 1825 is still on the house.

HAZEL: During that period, interest in urban renewal and historic preservation was just starting. With money from the renewal of my Radcliffe fellowship and the help of a friendly banker, we raised around $12,000 to buy the two houses, which were on the same lot. We also had all our valuables appraised and held an art sale to raise money.

I acted as the contractor, and we did a lot of the renovation ourselves. George rebuilt the fanlight around the front door; it had been destroyed and a corny little triangle put there. He revived the old rounded arc in a wonderful way. Then I did research on authentic colors. We painted the front house a soft olive green and the back house a Federal blue. Briand and I planted ivy and climbing roses.

When we bought the houses, we made a deal that we would never let owning a piece of property keep us from having a new adventure. It seemed very important at the time.

George had never owned a piece of property. It wasn't in his perspective. I remember when we had trees planted, George came home from teaching and stood watching the landscaping work. He shook his head and said, "I never thought I'd ever have to buy a tree."

GEORGE: An Indian buys a tree!

HAZEL: Do you remember when we went to Duluth for Christmas and stayed at your sister Josie's farm? There was very little heat in the house—that's why Josie wasn't staying there. She came over and made fires in the furnace for us.

Joe was 13 and Briand around 5. They got skates and we shoveled off the frozen lake. We cut down a Christmas tree, too, and brought it inside. Then, because we hadn't brought any ornaments, the kids and I made angels out of the tops of tin cans.

Josie cooked the turkey and everyone, all of George's family came. Your mother showed me how to make wild rice her way with onions, bacon grease, and lots of butter. Then I showed her how to make my pie crust. She always did like to watch me make pies.

HAZEL: Once when Briand was in kindergarten or first grade, a wonderful conversation occurred that shows how George and I and Briand operated as a family. George was driving, I was in the passenger seat, and Briand was hunched up between us. This was in the days before seat belts.

"Mother," Briand said, "do you believe in God?"

"Yes, I do."

Then Briand said to George, "Father, do you believe in God?"

George and I ended up having a discussion about God. Briand was right there between us, looking first at one, then at the other.

Finally, he said, "I didn't want to start anything. I just learned in school today that you can begin a conversation by asking a question."

Even as a young person, Briand didn't ask ordinary questions.

HAZEL: After we settled in Providence, I began teaching art full-time at the Lincoln School, a Quaker school for girls. Briand eventually went to the boys' companion school. It was good having him next door every day.

I remember some wonderful art shows at the Lincoln School. One in particular was on edible art. It involved students and other faculty and occurred at our house. Barbara Kruger, who taught with me, decided to reproduce one of George's "white paintings" in cream cheese sandwiches.

GEORGE: Not sandwiches. She made a sheet cake and frosted it with that cream cheese and powdered sugar mixture. That was the basic coloring for the white. Then she used food coloring to give the inflections of color underneath.

HAZEL: Well, we remember it differently. Anyway, as she worked, breaking the painting down mathematically to reproduce it, she found an amazingly perfect set of numbers repeated in spatial relationships across the canvas.

She was so excited that she brought in the head of the math department to look at it. The numbers weren't even—they were 11, 13, and so on. It was such an insight into an aesthetic, not imposed, but developed.

She made the edible version, then she froze it. The night of the show, she brought it into the house and set it down. One of George's students saw it and was appalled. "Don't let Professor Morrison see that or he'll have a fit." But he didn't. George was overwhelmed. He had not been aware of the mathematical relationships, but he said, "I'm not surprised."

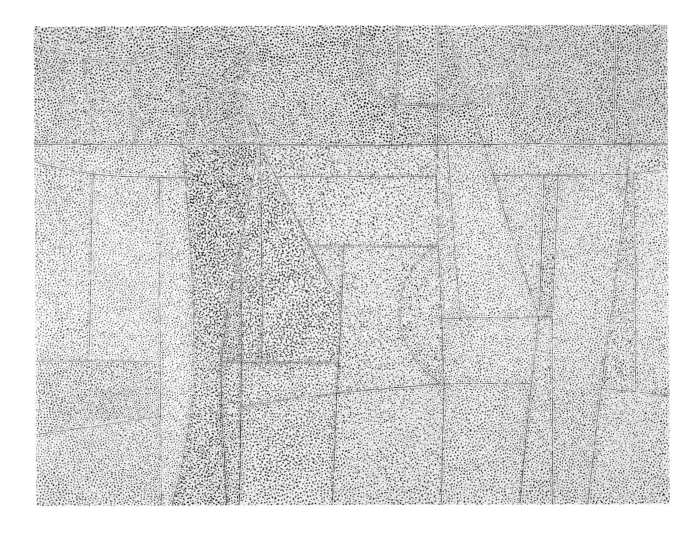

George's white paintings were the first works deliberately built up with layers and scumbling. He had worked this way before but never so intentionally. These paintings were a half-inch thick. White was the unifying factor, combining qualities of his drawings and paintings, more structural than many of his other works of the period.

The White Painting, 1971
Acrylic on canvas
46 x 60¾
Collection Heard Museum

GEORGE: In Providence I didn't show with a specific gallery, but I did have a one-man show and participated in group shows at the Rhode Island School of

Design. Then in Provincetown during the summer, I showed sometimes, and maybe in a gallery in Boston. But I was not specifically connected.

Leonard Boucour, a paint manufacturer in New York, bought a painting called *Paradial.* I had used a lot of his paints. The title refers to a parade— forms that are marching or staggering across the canvas. You can see the way the painting is leaning a little to the right. I think it comes from the way I walk, with one leg a little shorter than the other.

Another collector, Bayard Ewing, a very rich man and benefactor of the Rhode Island School of Design, also bought my work.

At the beginning of 1968, a group of artists from the Rhode Island School of Design had a show at Skidmore College in Saratoga Springs, New York. This gave Hazel and me an opportunity to exhibit together. She was teaching occasionally at the school. Remember, this was still the era when most so-called faculty wives were in their place, and the men were usually considered to have the dominant role in a relationship.

The show included my friend and colleague Jack Massey and also Alfred DeCredico, who had been my student. The reviewer, T. H. Littlefield, emphasized that the show brought together examples of Abstract Expressionism, hard-edge abstraction, and Pop Art in "an exciting show . . . full of vitality and wit and sprezzatura."

I was the Abstract Expressionist. "[R]ich, subtle depths," Littlefield said of my work. "Allusions keep emerging, to fenced lands, to houses, to headstone slabs, to wheels, to human anatomy. . . . pictures that feed the imagination." In Hazel's acrylics, especially the series *To Joe* and *From Joe,* Littlefield found a dialogue primarily of colors, and then of field and ground.

GEORGE: In 1969 I was granted an honorary Master of Fine Arts degree from the Minneapolis School of Art. They paid our way to attend the graduation ceremonies and treated us like dignitaries. It was a very nice honor.

Later that summer Briand and I came back to visit my mother, who was stricken with cancer.

Her death came just before Christmas. Briand remembers that she died just after many of the family had left, and the highway patrol had to stop them and send them back.

I don't remember the funeral except she was not buried in Chippewa City. The service must have been in Duluth, and she was buried in an ordinary cemetery there.

Converging of the Green: Fire Ridge

GEORGE: In 1970 I gave up my tenure-track position as associate professor at the Rhode Island School of Design. It was the first big job I had had, and it had been good. Providence was and still is a good art town, with the best art school in America. But it's easy to get lost in academia.

I wanted to come back to the Indian connection, to Minnesota and my family. I felt an inner need to come back, not realizing the consequences of what I was doing. I felt the need to put certain Indian values into my work.

There was a job opening at the University of Minnesota in a new program in American Indian studies. I applied. It turned out to be a dual appointment with the Studio Arts Department and the American Indian Studies Department. The Indian Studies course was a lecture course that met once a week like a seminar.

HAZEL: When the letter came accepting George, I wasn't that keen on the move. Both of us had good jobs—I had been teaching six years at the Lincoln School, and George had a full-time permanent job at the Rhode Island School of Design. But I knew that he had a rivalry in the department, and he really wanted to go back to Minnesota.

The main thing for me was that Joe, who had been living with us, had been so sick with leukemia. He had a good clinic in Providence; finally he had started to get better. Was this the time to move him?

1970–1983

Teaching American Indian studies and studio arts at the University of Minnesota

Another home renovation

Involvement with American Indian Movement

Era of wood collages

Shows and commissions

Health problems

Buying Red Rock

Retirement

The church house
in St. Paul, 1970.
Courtesy of Hazel Belvo

We also had just finished renovating the houses on Transit Street. Those were the minuses. I could think of one plus for Briand. It might be good for him to be around his Indian cousins, his Indian family, because we didn't know any Indian people in Providence. But I was worried that the job at the University of Minnesota was only a one-year appointment. That was risky.

So I said to George, "Let's ask Joe what he wants." Joe was fifteen. Despite being ill, he loved adventure. He said he would be happy to go.

All in just two weeks, George got the letter offering him the job, we had that discussion, and Joe said OK. In the second week I put the houses on Transit Street up for sale, and in three days I sold them. I was exhausted.

GEORGE: I went on ahead to Minnesota to look for a place to live, and right away, with the help of friends David and Ginny Bueide, I found an abandoned church, formerly Ascension Lutheran Church, on the corner of Cleveland and Stanford avenues in St. Paul. It was a stroke of luck. Nobody wanted it, and I got it for $30,000. Ten years later we sold it for $130,000. It even included the pews.

But it was not a conventional church with a spire—they had taken the cross off the top. It did not have colored windows, though the windows had a suggestion of Gothic. Still, it took a lot of work to get rid of the church part and make it livable.

HAZEL: Soon after we moved in, George and I had our familiar argument about wall space. "There are only so many walls," he would say, wherever we moved. When I would claim a wall, he would declare, "Hazel wants equal wall space."

George and I are a generation apart. In his generation, women didn't compete with their husbands—for careers or for wall space. He thought that when two artists married, one would inevitably do something secondary. I sometimes think that the difference in our ages had a bigger impact on our relationship than the difference in our culture.

GEORGE: We put a lot of money and work into that church. We covered it with wood siding to get away from the church look and converted the church hall in the basement into my studio and workshop. Hazel had a studio constructed upstairs, and we added redwood decks and a stairway going to the second floor.

For Briand's room, we put a ladder up one wall to a loft and I built a bed, with bookshelves, a desk, and chair, all built in. Then downstairs we built a wall to separate out a bedroom from the main area. We sanded and refinished the floors. It was a good place. Eventually the neighbors got used to having the old abandoned church turned into a house.

Artists tend to mold their environment wherever they live, I told a newspaper reporter at the time. Our personalities went into the house and were reflected in what was there.

I guess I still believe those things.

HAZEL: When we bought the church, we found an old upright piano left there. I took it apart, cleaned and repaired it, and painted it white. Then Briand started taking piano lessons. I had also given George a Guild guitar with the first paycheck I got from teaching.

My family had been "hill musicians" in southern Ohio; my grandmother led a band and never went silent a day in her life. George had played music as a teenager. Now he played the guitar. Joe also got good in guitar. Dan could play a banjo and so could I. But Briand became the real musician of us all, a gifted jazz musician.

The church was a beautiful place to live. Eventually, after ten years of living there, I had 187 plants.

GEORGE: I came back to teach at the University of Minnesota at just the right time. Indians were coming up in education. There wasn't much opportunity in the East. But various institutions in the West, from California to Minnesota, were forming Indian studies programs. It was the result of the civil rights movement of the '60s. The Indians picked it up after the blacks.

I began to be invited to various Indian studies departments—one in Missoula, Montana; then other institutions in Minnesota, including colleges like St. Olaf; and some colleges in Wisconsin—to give slide lectures of my work. I think introducing Indian art in a broad sense into the curriculum was a good idea.

These Indian studies programs helped to spur the American Indian Movement. AIM became well known and well thought of, politically, all over the country. Two Ojibway men founded it: Clyde Bellecourt and Dennis Banks. Bellecourt was an urban Indian from St. Paul, and Banks was from the Leech Lake area of Minnesota. They met in Stillwater prison where they were influenced by a young Ojibway spiritual leader, Edward Benton-Banai.

After they were released from prison, they inspired a group of young Indian men and women to patrol in red jackets along Franklin Avenue in Minneapolis. They called themselves the AIM patrol, and their goal was to protect Indians drinking in bars from police harrassment.

Though I didn't consider myself an activist—they protested, later going to Washington and confronting senators and Congress—I became a member of AIM and, with Hazel, did my bit by helping to raise money.

HAZEL: George and I had a big mailing list that I had developed as part of my business orientation. We sent out many letters for AIM. We held benefits and raised quite a lot of money.

GEORGE: The movement became national and that was good. It prompted Indians to be aware of their own political situation.

But AIM was held in check by the powerful federal government. There was that 1973 seige at Wounded Knee, South Dakota, where armed U.S. federal marshals surrounded a gathering of AIM and Lakota tribal members. The FBI was involved, too. It had become that intense.

Later the government prosecuted members of AIM in Minneapolis. Though the government essentially lost the first legal round, it kept after many of the leaders for a long time.

But AIM did not disintegrate; it picked up a lot of interest with Indian groups all over the country. Even later, on some of my trips down to the Southwest, I heard of Indian groups that were still relating to AIM.

GEORGE: In the Indian studies program, my course was titled "The Arts of the American Indian." I showed old and new art in slides that I got from the Heye

George in his studio/home, St. Paul, 1973.

Minneapolis Tribune

foundation in New York. They had thousands of art objects, mostly old. I interspersed those with contemporary works that were three-dimensional as well as pictorial or graphic, including my own.

I did a lot of research. I'm glad I did, too, because it helped my knowledge. I started building a library of my own, an Indian library I still have—around fifty books. When I look back on it now, I'm certainly glad that I broadened my scope about Indian art. Doing research and actually looking at objects.

I showed slides in class and then we talked about tribal arts from different sections of the country. Out of a class of thirty, I might have had six Indian students; there weren't many enrolled in the university as a whole—200 out of 45,000. And the Indian students were taking up different things—medicine, business, and other subjects. I think it was a valuable course for non-Indian as well as Indian students, introducing them to what was going on in American Indian art from pre-Columbian to the present.

One of the nice things I did for the course was have students make something connected with Indian art. The projects were their choice. One girl had her father, who was a big-game hunter, get her an elk hide. She skinned and treated it from scratch. (You know that the traditional ingredients for tanning included the brains of an animal.) Other students made headdresses and drums. Some painted designs like Western tribes used on tepee covers or clothing. Some collected quills or made beadwork. The projects got them interested, and they did research of their own.

Then at the end of the course, we had a big Indian meal at our house. The class prepared many different dishes, up to fifty dishes. Every one had to be indigenous—corn soup or something from the Southwest or from the Woodland tribes. Lots of wild rice, different kinds of meat—deer, moose, elk, rabbit, and fowl. Then there were all kinds of puddings, some made out of corn and maple syrup. The students got a big charge out of it.

I taught the course only one year. After that, there was an opening for a full-time, permanent position in the Studio Arts Department, teaching painting and drawing. I applied and was hired as an associate professor. Eventually I was promoted to full professor, and the work load was reduced to two days a week. Six hours a day for two days a week. That comprised my load for studio arts—painting and drawing.

Several Indian students took studio arts from me. Frank Bigbear Jr., an Ojibway from near Walker, Minnesota, is now an artist in his own right. Even when he was studying with me, he was on a track by himself. He did all kinds of things that worked in and out of American Indian themes. I own some of his work.

Kent Smith, now an associate professor of Indian studies at Bemidji State University, was another Indian student working with me toward a master's degree in art. He's a sculptor. I own a drawing of his that has a sculptural feeling. It doesn't represent any Indian theme, except very indirectly.

GEORGE: In 1972 the Walker Art Center and the Minneapolis Institute of Arts sponsored a show of American Indian art. It was interesting to see the range of work, from British Columbia to the Plains Indians, from the Southwest to the Northeast. Most of the 900 objects were fuctional. As an art critic wrote in the *Minneapolis Tribune,* the makers and users of these objects would have been "intrigued and puzzled . . . to see [their work] on display in a museum."

The newspaper also published interviews with some of us local Indian artists. Mine emphasized that I wasn't painting "buffalo, war dances or eagle feathers. . . . '[A]n Indian doesn't have to paint tipis to be an artist,'" I told the interviewer.

Then I read him a statement I had written: "I have never tried to prove that I was Indian through my art. . . . Yet, there may remain deeply hidden some remote suggestion of the rock whence I was hewn, the preoccupation of the textural surface, the mystery of the structural and organic element, the enigma of the horizon, or the color of the wind."

When I look back, I see that the newspaper placed me somewhere in the middle between local Indian artists who didn't want to show at American Indian exhibitions and those who, on their own terms, drew their imagery or inspiration directly from Indian life.

George assembling a wood
collage, 1973.

Courtesy of George Morrison

GEORGE: When I came back to Minnesota, I began in earnest with some of my wood ideas. From the standpoint of originality, I can't think of many other people making wood collages in the manner I do. I hope people don't take them as oddities. I think a respectful, knowledgeable person would know that they're paintings in wood, landscapes.

There's a chance element in them—taking driftwood or discarded wood and playing one piece against the other. Just as you might in a still-life painting, playing bigger areas like a tablecloth against small objects like fruit.

As in my abstractions, I selected colors at random for a given spot on the collage. I clustered little pieces of wood alongside bigger ones. But unlike the abstractions, the wood collages are clearly based on landscape.

The early collages from Provincetown and Providence and the early days in Minnesota are looser, made strictly from found wood. Some of the wood I had brought from the Atlantic Ocean, some I gathered from alleys and backyards.

My later collages were fitted together more precisely. For them, I started accumulating all kinds of wood again. I started to weather wood, too, selecting brand new pieces that had some knots in them or a particular kind of grain. I might sand the edges to look a little worn. Then I put the wood outside for six months or a year. It gradually turned gray and became a usable piece.

The first wood collage I made in St. Paul was leaning up against the studio wall when we were having a party one night. Sam Sachs, the director of the Minneapolis Institute of Arts, was there and took a look at it. I guess he thought it was good. "I'll have someone pick it up," he said. "We'd like to keep it for a while." They bought it shortly after that. They paid around $4,000 to $5,000. Not very much. But at the time I was glad to sell it and have it in a good collection.

HAZEL: Soon after we moved, I began teaching art at Saint Paul Academy. Once I asked George if I could bring my seventh and eighth grade classes to visit his studio. We each had studios, and their differences reflected the different ways we worked. I cannot begin working until all the surfaces are neat. George is not like that.

The day the classes visited, George had the materials for a wood collage spread around in his basement studio. He had said we could come down and look, but he didn't want anyone to touch anything.

I prepared the class to be on their good behavior. But when one boy asked me a question, he picked up a piece of wood, about an inch in diameter. After his question, I took the piece out of his hand and set it down. But I guess I didn't put it in the same place where it had been before.

When George went down to work that evening, he knew someone had moved that one piece.

There were other differences as well in the way we approached things. Sometime after we moved to the Twin Cities, a young man connected to George's family got in a fight at a party. Somebody put a knife through his heart.

We were called to the emergency room and waited for hours to see if he would survive. He did survive, and the experience gave me an insight into a difference in George's background and mine. George was upset, of course; it was hard on him to have this young man so critically hurt, but it wasn't as uncommon in his experience as it was in mine. For me, it was drastic.

I was also dealing with Joe's illness and, in 1972, his death. Hospitals were difficult places for me to enter.

GEORGE: I never did, ever in my life, make a living from my art. Teaching provided me with steady income, so I could work without having to depend on selling art. It's true that I sold some very large works. But in one year I might make $3,000, the next year $5,000. It went up and down; I couldn't depend on it.

I never had a gallery in the Twin Cities that acted as an agent. People heard about the collages through word of mouth probably—maybe saw one at an exhibition. Or a corporation would buy one, and that would prompt more sales. Some of the largest works were commissioned works.

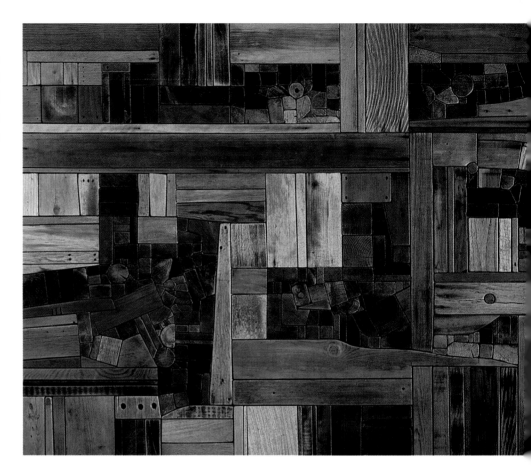

Cumulated Wood Landscape,
1976
Found and prepared wood
47 x 118
Collection Honeywell Corporation

The wood collages became kind of popular in the Twin Cities. I sold a lot of them to big corporations like Honeywell, Prudential, and General Mills, and Prudential later donated theirs to the Minnesota Historical Society. I call them major works because they are big—three by eight feet, four by ten feet, or, in the case of the collage at the art institute, five by fourteen feet. At the time, in the '70s and early '80s, they were priced at $2,000 to $4,000. Still not enough income to get by on.

It's strange but I still don't have a wood collage of my own. They have always been done on commission, on demand. Whenever I finished a piece, it was already sold. I'd like to come to the point where I could have one for myself. I suppose, if I went at it, I could finish one in a month, putting in time every day.

Usually I start at the lower left-hand corner, then work across and up. I put sizable pieces on the corners. You wouldn't want a little chip of wood there; it might break off. It must be substantial at the corners.

In the meantime, I draw a pencil line for the horizon. If the collage is four feet high, the line is a foot from the top. I might have a piece of wood that comes right up to that line, then I stop. The next piece will have a thin space in between. All the wood pieces have these little spaces between them which gives the illusion of a carved, incised line around each of them.

Using my sense of proportion, I vary thin pieces with wide ones, long with round.

It's interesting what you do and don't use. I decide, maybe not even consciously, that I won't use certain pieces, but I will use others of a different quality. The grain is always important. And the coloring of the wood—some is natural, some prepared by myself.

Whether I'm preparing wood to use later or selecting pieces for a work in progress, there's constant repetition of sizes. Some pieces run the length or height of the entire piece; they may be cut deliberately that way. These main proportions, repeated here and there, relate the parts to the whole. And that makes the piece more appealing.

Patricia Hobot, a Lakota who was gallery director at the Minneapolis American Indian Center, said this about my wood collages: "People often want something that is stereotypical Indian and involves racial stereotyping, . . . but George's work embodies the abstract values of the Indian people. . . . His use of pieces to make up a whole is very Indian. It shows respect for individuality but indicates how the individual is expected to fit into the whole." Those were good connections she made.

HAZEL: When the art institute had a show of collages, what interested me was their differences in character. You wouldn't have been aware of that if you hadn't seen them together. Seeing them all at once in the big gallery space was remarkable.

Each had such a distinct personality, even the new ones made of new wood, the more crafted wood. Yet there was a common spirit running through all of them. Our friend, the potter and sculptor Bob Jewett, said he finally understood George's work when he took some students sailing around Lake Superior. Everywhere he looked around the shore, he saw George's drawing, or painting, or collage.

GEORGE: The basis of all art is nature; it creeps in even to abstract art. The look of the North Shore was subconsciously in my psyche, prompting some of my images.

A lot of people like the collage owned by the art institute because they are attracted to wood. I imagine that people see the wood first. They don't look at it as a landscape painting, though it's subtitled *Landscape.* They may not even see the horizon line at first. The initial appeal comes from the wood itself, from the tactile surface.

The last time I saw that collage—coming in close and even touching some of the pieces—I was glad to see it was in fairly good condition after twenty years. The wood won't last forever, I know that. On occasion, I have told people who have ordered wood collages to put them under glass to protect them. But that seems wrong and they never do it.

Now that the art institute has redone its Native American galleries, they've hung my big collage in a fine spot. My friend Louise Lincoln, curator for the installation, told me that the museum chose the color of the gallery—a light bluish-gray—to complement the tones of my collage.

It was very interesting to see, at the beginning of the exhibit, my big collage with what I call my *Red Totem,* borrowed from the Art Institute of Chicago. Then at the end of the galleries was my *Churinga.* I feel very good about that.

GEORGE: In 1974 the Walker Art Center had a show of forty-five of my pen-and-ink drawings. These were big drawings, two feet square, done on fine Strathmore paper. They took my interest in texture and over-all design to a more pure and formal state than did the wood collages. I laid out the drawings with precise straight and curved lines, all the same distance apart. This gave the surface an even texture. Then I put the horizon line one-quarter from the top. I wanted to make that line very evident.

The Cubist element was there, too, in the breaking down of earlier landscape themes. And Surrealism in the idea of making an impression on the paper, either with paint or scribbles, then drawing in and around the accidental effects until certain images began to appear. Oddly enough, one of the drawings represents a tree coming through from the bottom to the top of the drawing. That was very subconscious.

Philip Larson, who wrote about the drawings for the catalog, said some of the drawings reminded him of "interwoven hair, inlaid floors, basketry." I said I saw a remote suggestion of Aztec architecture, but I wasn't looking for that.

I have always maintained that drawings can be major artworks. It was good to see this work from the previous four years displayed together.

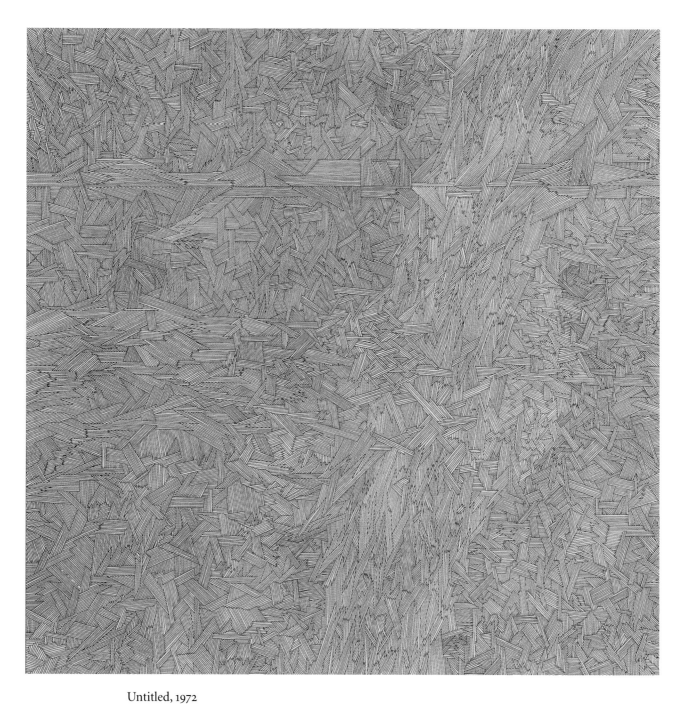

Untitled, 1972
Black ink on Strathmore paper
23 x 23
Collection Walker Art Center,
Minneapolis. Purchased with matching
grant from Museum Purchase Plan,
NEA, 1973

HAZEL: In 1974 George and I each had a show opening around Valentine's Day. The night of the openings we had a party to celebrate. We rented a place downtown and invited all the artists we knew. George was so sick when we were putting this together that I wanted him to go to the doctor. But he said he wasn't going to call the doctor because they would only put him in the hospital. Finally I made him promise that he would call the day after the opening.

Luckily, friends at the Mayo Clinic got George in right away. The next day he had surgery. It was peritonitis. If they hadn't operated, he would have died.

After this, George started talking about moving up north.

GEORGE: By the time we moved back to the Twin Cities, none of my family was living in Chippewa City. It had become nonexistent as a village. But in my mind, the village was an extension of the reservation.

During the years I lived out east, I had not stayed in connection with the tribe, had more or less given it up over the years. But now Hazel and I began to go up to visit the Witch Tree and stay by the lake. The lake has certain magical qualities for me in the sense that I like to be near it. To be part of it.

Over the years, Hazel had become very interested in the Witch Tree—the Spirit Little Cedar Tree, as the people call it. She appreciated its spiritual connection and began using the tree as a theme for many big works. She used tobacco juice for brown coloring and vermilion for reddish color. She made many kinds of images—prints, paintings, large drawings.

HAZEL: I had seen the Witch Tree for the first time around 1962. I was still carrying Briand in my arms then. We had the two bigger boys with us, too; Danny was around five, and Joe, eight. I'll never forget seeing the tree; it was so moving.

We went right down to the tree, and I had to watch that the children didn't hurt it, or slip and fall into the lake. George tore up a cigarette and gave some to Joe and Dan to make an offering in the Indian manner. Joe did it right away, but Danny said, "That's ridiculous." As we were leaving, I turned. There was Danny with his back to the tree and his arms behind him, throwing out the tobacco. He was not going to take a chance.

Over the years we have visited the Spirit Little Cedar Tree countless times.

This 400-year-old tree, growing out of lichen-covered rock above the lake, has for me the presence and feeling of a cathedral. It has become one of the primary images in my work. The tree is for me what the horizon is for George.

GEORGE: I painted the tree once in acrylic and did drawings of it in my journal. Neither of us painted directly from the tree. Hazel made little sketches there at the tree but, by and large, she worked at home. She's a studio painter, like myself.

Now, I was thinking of returning to my home area, the reservation in Grand Portage. Many times, it's interpreted that coming back home is making the full circle. Coming around. I suppose I really wanted to get home again. As to why, I don't know. I guess there's a natural attraction to where you were born, your locale. Like the lake or the woods for me.

Over the years, my family had owned parts of the reservation, which were handed down. The allotment act said Indians could do whatever they wanted with the land allotted to them. Regrettably, many of them sold it for whatever they could get. My family sold theirs back to the reservation, which was a good thing. It was land way back in the woods, without easy access, but it had some value in timber and mineral resources.

Tribal land is available for any enrolled member of the Grand Portage band. You can take your choice of any available land on the reservation. But now you can't sell it; you can only use it. It can be yours for a lifetime, but you have to build on it and prove that you're using it properly.

When I wanted to get land on the lake, Hazel and I looked around at several spots on the reservation. We stayed at the lodge at Grand Portage until we found the section of lakeshore we called Red Rock. I liked it because it was rather private and interesting.

HAZEL: A young Indian spiritual leader once said to me, "When your magic appears to you, you will recognize it." When George finally stood on Red Rock, he knew it was the place. I stood next to a tall black spruce and said, "This is where our front door will be." Red Rock, we learned later, is jasper, George's mineral on the medicine wheel. The black spruce is my plant totem.

GEORGE: The studio at Red Rock started very modestly—just a little cabin that we moved from Grand Marais to the property. Then we had a road built from scratch.

HAZEL: Danny and I cut down the trees with a power saw. George hired a friend from Hovland to move the cabin, bulldoze the lot, and grade and finish the road.

GEORGE: Around this time the Minneapolis American Indian Center was beginning to take shape. Ron Libertus, a Chippewa from the White Earth Reservation and a member of the Indian Art Association that had cosponsored the 1972 exhibit with the Walker and the art institute, was also a leader in developing the center. The Chippewa tribe of Minnesota, plus Indian organizations in Minneapolis, and maybe even federal government monies for Indians—all helped to finance the building. Ron helped me get a National Endowment for the Arts grant of $10,000 to design a facade for the building.

The building design was a good one, done by Hodne architectural partners, of Minneapolis, which had included some young Indian architects on their staff. Hazel and I were friends with Tom Hodne and got to know the young Indian architects as well. I thought it was smart to have hired them, not only because they were Indian but also because they were young architects on their way to becoming good.

My design for the facade was taken from a feather. I think all Indians have connections to birds and their feathers, using them in symbolic ways. My sources were varied, inspired by chevron shapes. When you look at my design, with its geometric form, it isn't a realistic rendering of a feather, but it derives from the feather.

I drew the design on paper first. Then the carpenters followed the plan, using cedar boards in the same standard widths as they used for the sides of the building. They didn't have to cut the boards except where the chevrons met or stopped. The way the wood is placed gives the illusion that some of the chevrons are turning around. Some are going one way and some the

Untitled Collage, 1974–1975
(1997 photo)
Wood construction
216 x 1,176
Minneapolis American Indian Center
Photo by Jerry Mathiason

other. In the center, they come together and form something that is almost three-dimensional. The turning around is an optical illusion; you can't explain it.

The wood was not weathered initially. It became weathered in time, some darker and some lighter. This has added to the illusion of movement across the surface.

The mural was dedicated at the opening ceremonies in 1975. Strangely enough, I had a dream that coincided with Indian Week when the center opened. Indian Week is always the first part of May. In my dream, one of the

features was a vast field of feathers. Later I did a painting called *I Dream of a Feathered Field.*

The dream and the mural were twenty years ago. Now the mural needs refurbishing. People don't seem to care about the Indian center. They probably just think the mural is the side of the building. They don't understand that it originated as a work of art.

Who is there to take care of it but myself? I want to have it resurfaced and stained with a reddish stain to give a little more emphasis to the design. There's a color called Indian Red that is close to burnt sienna. That would be a nice color to add, then apply lacquer to protect it. I'd like to put in spotlights and have a plaque made for the mural that states it is an original work of art. It would be nice to call it *Turning the Feather Around.* A mural for the Indian.

Soon after I finished the mural, I was selected by the Daybreak Star arts center in Seattle to do another one. The Daybreak Star center, like the Indian center here, was very nice. Their tract of land was generously donated by the City of Seattle. It was unique, in the shape of a star.

I had been to Seattle a few times to share my slides and meet some of the Indians there. Then, via a competition, they selected Indians from different parts of the country to create designs for the center. I was selected to represent Woodland Indians, and I was to use a theme related to that.

I did some research and created an indoor mural called *The Underwater Panther.* That theme is common with the Woodland Indians, who claim there are spirits living in the water; some of the spirits are referred to as underwater panthers. My design was semiabstract: two panthers facing each other, done in redwood, with maybe three colors of wood.

GEORGE: I think the original meaning of Indian art begins with tribal meanings. A lot of Indian sculptures had a religious or spiritual meaning. Coming back to Minneapolis made my mark in a new way because I got involved with the Indian thing again—like joining AIM, designing murals for the Indian centers, being a little bit active in Indian affairs. And I began developing three-dimensional totems. It all came around, almost developed by itself, but also with the dictates of my own head. It all came around—that's a good way of putting it.

My totems were monumental in scale.

Totem is a Chippewa word that means "family mark." Totemic imagery may be common to native peoples all over the world. Such vertical structures are found in the Taula forms in Minorca, linga structures in India, Stonehenge in England, and those of the ancient Olmecs in Mexico.

Opposite:
Totem, 1979
Stained wood
144 x 15 x 15
Collection Tweed Museum of Art,
University of Minnesota, Duluth
Sax Brothers Purchase Fund

The Northwest Coast Indians also made monumental totems, carved from their colossal trees. But they didn't call them art. Their totems meant for them a kind of wealth. For instance, a man would prove his wealth by engaging a carver to make a totem, decorating it with animals that were part of the patron's totemic history, his connection to the animal world. They made small poles for houseposts and gravestones and larger ones to display prominently in their settlements.

Unlike the totems of the Northwest Coast Indians, my totems were not for outdoors; the weather would have destroyed them. My totems were also square, not round. And I didn't use animal images on them. I did my own abstract interpretation.

My first totem resulted from an invitation in 1977 from Evan Maurer, now director of the Minneapolis Institute of Arts, who was then curator of the department of African, Oceanic, and Native American art at the Art Institute of Chicago. He asked different Indian artists to submit work for a show he was putting together. We could do anything we wanted. I did my first totem.

I made it the size of the plywood I could get, ten feet tall. The height gave it a certain monumentality. The totem isn't solid; it's hollow. If it were solid, it would be monstrously heavy. Even with pieces of plywood appliqued to a core, it became heavy enough.

The appliques were my imitations of carving. I was thinking of Mayan and Olmec columns from 1000 A.D., which are chiseled chunks of stone. My design is very precise, with the shapes locked around corners. It's also very angular in the sense that there are only straight lines, no curves. It's kind of Constructivist, like Mondrian and Moholy-Nagy. Straight edges, flat shapes.

It's made of redwood, stained all one color. I chose a red earth color called Indian Red to assimilate a certain Indianness because, otherwise, it's just a modern, abstract version of a totem pole. When Evan Maurer wrote the blurb for the catalog, he called the red stain "an allusion to the sacred earth paint." He got the feeling of what I was trying to do.

Some artists want to make the whole thing themselves, but I'm not able to because of my physical disabilities. So I engaged some students from the

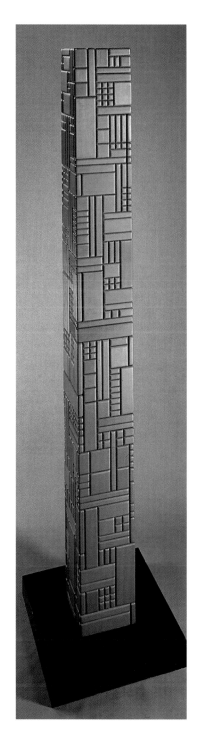

Minneapolis College of Art and Design to build the totem, and they did the work there in the college facilities. I feel that if I design something and it's pretty much followed to a T, then that's okay.

The Chicago art institute eventually bought the totem from their show for $6,000, not very much by standards now. But here again, I was glad to get it. Because the totem was already at the museum, I didn't have to pay storage, packing, delivering, returning. And I appreciated the honor of being in a good collection.

HAZEL: With George and me, there was so much commonality from our commitment to art; it was intellectually inspiring. I remember hearing a Native American female anthropologist speak at a Chippewa powwow in Duluth. She listed the values of Native American culture on one side of the board and those of Euro-American culture on the other. The only place they overlap, she said, is in feminism.

By then, the middle '70s, I was very involved in the feminist art movement with the WARM, Women's Art Registry of Minnesota, gallery and other programs. Hearing her say this made clear why I felt so close to George's culture. Yet George had taken on the intellect and practice of white male culture, as well. It was complex.

Visiting George's friend, the artist Jaune Quick-To-See Smith, also helped me understand what my position was. Jaune is a Flathead/Cree/Shoshoni from Montana. Like the women in George's family, she was very friendly and gracious to me. Do you remember, George, what she said when she met me? "Why, George, the way you described her, I expected her to be wearing combat boots."

She and I talked feminism, art, and activism until four in the morning. We also talked about cultural differences. She told me how Indian women felt about my being white and married to a prominent Indian man. I understood that they might resent it. But I was a lot like pioneer women, she said, with an orientation to land and life similar to Indian women. That also helped explain what George and I had together.

I remember the first time George's sister asked me to dance at a powwow. She and a group of other woman danced over to me. It was about ten years after George and I were married. I never felt I could push my way in. I knew it would take a while. I waited and listened, and eventually I felt completely accepted.

GEORGE: In 1979 Hazel and I went to Havana, Cuba, on a cultural exchange. We were with a group of Native American artists that included Frank LaPena and Oren Lyons, one of my Iroquois friends, and another friend from the Onondaga tribe who taught at the State University of New York near Syracuse. Frank is a California Indian, of the Nomtipom subdivision of the Wintu tribe—a dancer and singer and a good painter. His Spanish name suggests the intermarriage of Spanish and Indians in that area.

At the time there was no direct flight between the U.S. and Cuba. We went through Montreal and took a Russian plane from there to Havana.

I took slides with me and gave lectures about my work. Our art was on exhibit at the Casa de las Americas. Then we went sight-seeing in Havana, a very beautiful city. The Cubans treated us to good food and entertained us as first-class visitors.

HAZEL: For George's 60th birthday that September, we gave a big party at the church. I asked Bob Rose Bear to carve a pipe with an eagle for George. There was a big ceremony; I had asked George not to drink until afterwards. Finally around 2:00 or 3:00 A.M. when things quieted down, I realized he didn't look good. He had dark circles around his eyes. From watching his mother when she was ill, I knew that this was a family characteristic.

The next morning Briand and I left for school not knowing what would happen. When we returned, we learned that George had driven himself to the Mayo Clinic and was in the critical care unit. He had had a heart attack.

GEORGE: I've been plagued by health setbacks since I was ten, when they discovered TB of the hip.

Hospital Lobby, St. Mary's, Rochester, Minn.—10.22.1979
Pencil on paper
10⅝ x 8⅛
Collection Minnesota Historical Society

In the 1970s I struggled with stomach problems, partly the result, I suppose, of bad diet and alcoholism. During one Mayo Clinic stay, I had a biopsy of my stomach and intestine. The doctors did surgery; they took out a lot of the intestine. Luckily, this was just in time. They got the cancer before it could attack the other organs.

Later I had an aneurysm in my aorta. The doctors at the Mayo Clinic put in a Teflon tube to fix it. I tell people I'm running on spare parts.

HAZEL: After he had the heart attack, George wanted to move up north more permanently. The lake attracted him, of course. He wanted to enlarge the little cabin and make studios for both of us on the lake.

We tried to keep the church house, which we both loved; we thought we could make an apartment or two in it to help defray the high taxes. But the neighborhood objected.

Then, one day as I was leaving a meeting at the art institute, I saw a big sign across Stevens Avenue. An old house was going to be sold at auction—a famous house called the Stebbins House that had gone to seed. We decided to have our friend, the architect Tom Hodne, renovate it. We moved in in 1980.

Meanwhile, George was building the studios up north. I remember drawing a plan that incorporated the cabin and added two big studios, one for him on a lower level, and one for me on a third level, with living area in the middle. Then George implemented it. He had the credibility necessary to hire workmen on the reservation; workmen up there wouldn't talk to a woman.

I was still very attached to Cape Cod and Provincetown. For many summers after we moved to Minnesota, I had continued to rent the downstairs of 8 Law Street. Then the house came up for sale. I wanted to buy it with a good friend who had lived upstairs. But I realized I couldn't do that and also contribute to building the studios at Grand Portage. I had to make the difficult choice.

So I sold my share to another close friend and tried to put all my interest up north.

George and I were trying to hold onto our romantic, creative ideal. Both of our lives were centered around art—teaching art, making art. But the extent of our relationship at this time was really just our public selves.

George and Hazel at
Lake Superior, 1986
St. Paul Pioneer Press and Dispatch
(Joe Rossi)

GEORGE: While I was recuperating from the heart attack, I started making several small paintings that I eventually called the Horizon series. I had been working in larger scale, usually with assistants, on wood collages. But it was easier for me to do small canvases. I could work at a table in a more relaxed manner.

HAZEL: The format for these small paintings came out of New York. When we walked the New York streets, we would find wood, bring it home, cut it to

Landscape: Wood Collage
(*The River*), 1983
Prepared and stained wood
48 x 240
Collection University of
Minnesota Law School
Given in memory of Julius E. Davis
by the Dean E. Smith and
Julius E. Davis families

good right angles, then glue canvas scraps on the surface, and so have a good base for small paintings. George made a stack of these while the big studios at Grand Portage were being built.

GEORGE: By the early '80s, I was being invited to submit work to exhibits of contemporary Indian art. And museums that specialized in Indian work bought mine. The Philbrook got my painting *The Badlands*, from 1981.

Earlier definitions of Indian art—art based on recognizable tribal imagery, painted in the flat decorative style popular at the Santa Fe Indian School—were changing. For a long time, if you didn't paint like that, people had trouble considering you an Indian artist.

My friend Jamake Highwater included me in his book *The Sweet Grass Lives On.* I took the book with me when I traveled to the Southwest in the next decade and collected signatures when I met the artists. The book was dedicated to Yeffe Kimball, my friend in New York, who had passed away.

It was also good to exhibit my work—a totem—with Indian friends like

Jaune Quick-To-See Smith and Frank LaPena in a show called "Confluences of Tradition and Change: 24 American Indian Artists," organized in 1981 at the University of California, Davis. I even went to Davis to speak about my totem in that show. You could say I was looking for new directions.

GEORGE: Nearing retirement from the University of Minnesota, I got a commission for a huge wood collage for the university's law school from the family of Julius Davis. I used imported woods—ebony, cherry, padauk, walnut, oak—in very refined shapes.

Along the way, the river came to mind—the Mississippi River runs by the school. When that happened, I let the lighter wood come through the center and move in and out like a river with all its little tributaries and inlets. The horizon line is there, of course, one-quarter from the top. That's the signature of my paintings and collages.

I consider it a major work. But it's in a kind of dark hallway at the law school so it's not seen very well. Someday I'd like it to be in a more visible spot. Maybe it could be installed in the Frederick R. Weisman Art Museum at the university. That would be an ideal place for it, right above the river.

HAZEL: In the early '80s, we had a devastating trip back to Provincetown. That had become a drinking and partying place for George before we left the East Coast. He did not work there anymore. But I wanted to go back because even in the summers with my children, I had always gotten a lot of painting and drawing done there.

So the year I had a sabbatical from teaching at Saint Paul Academy, I first worked in a loft in New York. Then in the summer George picked me up, and we drove to Provincetown to spend a couple of weeks.

Briand, who was in college at the Berklee College of Music in Boston, was there, too, camping in the trailer park in Provincetown.

GEORGE: From my own experience with a lot of social drinking in New York, Providence, and Minneapolis, and heavy drinking back when I was a kid in Chippewa City, I realized that Briand was into the drinking thing. Maybe I criticized him for it; I was already in it and I probably thought I could understand it better than he could.

Drinking comes from an environment. At the Rhode Island School of Design, then in Minnesota, we were always having parties and having people to dinner, where we served drinks and wine. Social drinking, I call it.

But it was easier for me to take drinking to excess because I grew up in the Chippewa City environment where my father and neighbors did a lot of drinking. My mother never drank. Since drinking was part of the way of life, I accepted it as such.

HAZEL: After that visit to Provincetown, I wanted to change my life. In 1982 we all went into treatment for alcohol and drug addiction. It was good for all three of us. A lot got said.

GEORGE: Hazel and I were supportive; we went in for twenty-eight days. Briand did pretty well, but Hazel followed the program right down the line. She stopped and never drank again. I went back to it gradually, not as a hard-core alcoholic, but having a glass of wine with friends, having liquor on hand to offer guests.

I went to AA only for the twenty-eight days of the treatment, but it was valuable even if it didn't have an immediate effect. Though I occasionally drink now, I'm not the alcoholic I was in high school and college and later.

Alcoholism happens to a lot of families, as it did to us. These things have to be said.

GEORGE: When I retired from the university in 1983, I was honored with a one-man show at the University Gallery, "George Morrison: Entries in an Artist's Journal." Lyndel King, director of the gallery, was the prime mover behind it. The exhibit was a good way to end my formal teaching career. Drawing has always created a dialogue between myself and my students, and their responses often inspired me.

Working together, Lyndel and I selected pages from my journals spanning my career. It was like putting my private diary on public display.

I've always been a drawer—doodling, carrying sketchbooks wherever I went. Throughout my career the sketchbook or journal has been an intimate source of personal expression—first as a means of social narration and place description, then as a means of probing the subconscious through Surrealist and automatic drawing techniques to record an inner solitude and loneliness.

In the journal pages I always labeled time and place. In the show you could thus trace my moves from New York to Paris, Provincetown, Dayton, Grand Portage, and the Twin Cities. To Havana, Cuba; Sandpoint, Idaho, where I installed a totem;

Briand and George in Provincetown, 1978.
Courtesy of Hazel Belvo

to Montreal; Mariposa, California; Window Rock, Arizona; and Chimayo, New Mexico.

A few of the journal drawings were sketches for later works, but as Lyndel noted, the majority were finished works in themselves.

The show included pages of quotations from my journals—everything from the gravestone of Rin Tin Tin, a Craig Claiborne recipe for poached salmon, and a fortune from Hazel's fortune cookie, to lines from Emerson, Thoreau, Coleridge, John Dewey, Anne Sexton, Shakespeare, Dee Brown, Tecumseh, Whitman, William Carlos Williams, Camus, Michael Dennis Browne, Oscar Wilde, Man Ray, Georgia O'Keeffe, Kandinsky, Matisse, Delacroix, and El Greco. I liked the way Lyndel King called these quotations "stream-of-consciousness poetry."

One of my favorite journal fragments I wrote in 1982. It's a kind of homage to Fra Andrea Pozzo, a seventeenth-century Italian painter known for the ceiling of St. Ignatius church, in Rome:

> . . . sometimes, at an opportune time when there happened to be an opening in the sky—usually a light beautiful blue surrounded by soft white clouds—it would immediately remind me of looking thru the clouds toward heaven, as in the illusion at St. Ignatius Church in Rome which we visited in 1976. Of course it was the grand illusion of the Baroque architects, sculptors and painters, who by height, scale and intense realism gave the feeling of actual angels sculpted on the edges of the ceiling . . . [ascending] towards . . . heaven. It is that awesome combination of fear, wonder and revelation through religion and art. We always referred to that particular sky as the "Pozzo sky". . . .

Now my journals are all disbanded. Some pages are Xeroxed. All are mixed up here in these piles. I want to assemble them in appropriate ways to display them, yet keep them together as a group of works.

I'm still drawing now, using colored pencil. I don't keep a drawing pad by the bed, but I always have one on hand somewhere.

CEREMONY INTO THE LIGHT: ORACLE

GEORGE: In September 1986 several newspapers in the region wrote about me. They said I was dying of Castleman's disease, a lymph system disorder. Yes, I had the disease, but here you see me today, almost ten years later. It hasn't been easy.

As I recall, I was very sick and weak. A complete lack of energy.

HAZEL: I was at an opening in New York in 1984 when George got sick. The clinic in Grand Marais sent him to the hospital in Duluth. We didn't know what was the trouble. I took him home to the apartment in St. Paul. We had bought a smaller condo on Grand Avenue after selling the Stebbins House in Minneapolis to raise money for the studios up north.

GEORGE: Eventually I entered the oncology service at the University of Minnesota Hospital, where my doctor made the diagnosis. Castleman's disease is a rare condition; only several cases exist in the medical journals, and those patients usually have died within thirty months.

I was treated with chemotherapy, radiation, and prednisone, a powerful drug. Then I was released from the hospital. Bob Jewett, our artist friend from Saint Paul Academy, and Rob Woutat, another SPA teacher, brought me from the hospital to the apartment, one on each arm.

Once a week, I went back to continue the treatments. I don't know how long that lasted.

1984–1996

Castleman's disease

Recuperation in St. Paul and Grand Portage

Healing ceremony

Horizon paintings

Chiringa Forms

Retrospective and other shows

Decision to divorce

Living in Grand Portage

HAZEL: When we found out what George had, I arranged to take a year's leave of absence from the art department at Saint Paul Academy. The best place for George to heal was Red Rock, but he had to have home care and I couldn't get anyone up there to care for him. George had a good remission the first summer, and we established a routine. Get up and work, break for lunch and work some more, then break for dinner. Afterwards, George would read and I'd do some drawing.

Our friend Joanne Hart wrote about us and our work at Grand Portage for the *Lake Superior Magazine.* She described our studios, George's on the ground floor and mine above, and our living space, "white-walled to display their large collection of contemporary art, filled with light from raised ceiling and big windows that bring the broad expanse of Superior into their living-dining area."

She also mentioned work we had in the tenth-anniversary show of the Minnesota Artists Exhibition Program at the Minneapolis Institute of Arts—work we had created in homage to Lake Superior. George showed some of his small Horizon paintings, and I showed my two *Torsos* from my *Witch Tree: Spirit Cedar* series.

GEORGE: In the winter of 1986, I landed back in the hospital.

HAZEL: The same hospitals, the same doctors—it had happened to me when Joe died, and it was happening again, thirteen years later with George.

GEORGE: When I first heard about this disease, I got scared. Luis Buñuel, the Spanish film director, said, "The only trouble I have now is old age." Henry Miller said something like that, too. They get old and they want to keep going. I wanted to keep going.

But you have to realize that your time does run out sooner or later. This was seventeen months after the onset of the disease; if it followed the usual course, I didn't have much longer to live.

I started to think about summing up my life, about legacies, to document the work I'd done and find out where it went.

I wanted to work on more sculptural ideas and do more drawings. I wanted to have a big show, a lifetime show that would pull my work together. I didn't know if I would have the time.

Red Rock, George's studio/home on the shores of Lake Superior, Grand Portage Reservation.

Courtesy of George Morrison

HAZEL: In the spring of 1986, Walter Caribou gave George his Indian names in an intimate, powerful healing ceremony. "[Walter] spoke of the responsibility in giving," I wrote later, "that George now has a special position in Walter's life; the giver is careful in bestowing names; that the name must be learned and spoken daily so the named will know his name. Walter then spoke of his dream [in which the two names had come to him]. George has two names of equal importance to him and his journey."

When I heard those names, I understood their connection to George and his work.

GEORGE: The ceremony took place at the Grand Portage house. Walter insisted on food being present, so Hazel made some fry bread and fish. They were part of the ceremony; we each took a little.

One of the novices, Billy Blackwell, also was there. He was studying to become an interpreter of the Indianness of the reservation.

It wasn't a step-by-step ceremony. Walter did some chanting and some Indian singing and said some of his own prayers in Chippewa. Then he gave me my two Indian names and two eagle feathers.

HAZEL: When my year in Grand Portage was over, I hated to leave the peace. In winter it is the most beautiful place in the world.

When I returned to St. Paul, George came with me. The condo had a small basement that I converted into a studio. As George was recovering from recurrent bouts of the Castleman's disease, I encouraged him to continue working. I had learned from helping my son Joe during his leukemia treatments that making plans helps. I thought it would do George good to have a goal.

GEORGE: I started working at the table where we had our meals. I made many of the small Horizon paintings there.

I used scraps of three-quarter-inch plywood that I cut into convenient little shapes, usually horizontal. I mounted raw canvas on the board with glue and set weights on it, then let it dry overnight. The next day I trimmed it and gessoed the canvas with white gesso, which is like a chalky kind of paint. I let that dry overnight. Then it was ready to paint.

HAZEL: One day I put some of George's Horizon paintings in a shopping bag and went to see Jim Czarniecki, director of the Minnesota Museum of Art. Jim liked the paintings and talked about having an exhibit of them the next year.

GEORGE: When I could, I went back up north.

Through my windows at Grand Portage, I can see the lake change by the hour, from blue to yellow and rose. Dramatic things happen in the sky, with clouds and color. A rough spot appears on the water way off in the distance, or very, very rough water starts toward shore, or a streak of light illuminates the horizon. The ways I respond to these changes are both subconscious and perceptual.

The phenomenon of the clouds and other images from nature—pebbles or rocks or trees on the beach—all come right in these windows. I don't look at them as I paint, but they enter the paintings and I interpret them in an abstract way.

George in his Red Rock studio, 1993.

Photo by Marlene Wisuri

The basic thing in all the paintings is the horizon line which identifies each little work as a broad expanse of a segment of the earth.

I always start working below and above the horizon line. I put tape over the top of the canvas and work on the bottom. The next time around, I might tape the bottom and work on the sky.

I use the tape to get a clean line at the horizon. Sometimes I even put tape on both sides so I can paint a thin pencil-width line all the way across. I usually paint that line red—it becomes the horizon line at a given time of day, probably sunrise or sunset. I use that brilliant line, right at the edge, quite a lot. It's one of my painter's tricks.

In the Horizon series I have interpreted nature predominantly with my colors, primary colors—the artist's prerogative to choose his own colors.

The color range is exaggerated, but I have sometimes used a muted palette to catch a range of light after sunrise or before sunset.

One thing that makes the little paintings vibrant is the layering of colors. I might start with red, then stipple on the opposite or complement of that, blue, then come back to red, then another cold color. The color way underneath comes through to the surface and gives the sensation of shimmering movement.

It's the same with anything in nature—light hitting a rock, then bouncing against the water. The shimmer is nature coming through.

One of the notions in my imagination was to capture the infinite variations and changes of moods that pass over the lake at different times.

I am fascinated with ambiguity, change of mood and color, the sense of sound and movement above and below the horizon line. Therein lies some

Landscape/Seascape with Surrealist Forms: Red Rock Variation, 1984
Pen and ink and pencil on paper
2½ x 7¼ (image only)
Collection Minnesota Historical Society

of the mystery of the paintings: the transmutation, through choosing and manipulating the pigment, that becomes the substance of art.

HAZEL: The years when George was sick and went back and forth from St. Paul to Grand Portage were awkward years for our relationship. Not awkward privately but publicly, because the public romanticized us. Certainly, George was romanticized partly because of his heritage, and we both were treated this way because we were fun, creative, and colorful people. But the truth was we had our individual lives. I had my friends and colleagues at the WARM gallery and Saint Paul Academy, then at the Minneapolis College of Art and Design where I became associate professor and head of fine arts. I continued to have my friends in New York and Provincetown. George had another circle.

Red Rock Crevices. Soft Light.
Lake Superior Landscape, 1987
Acrylic and ink on canvas on board
6½ x 11½
Collection Tweed Museum of Art,
University of Minnesota, Duluth
Alice Tweed Tuohy Foundation Purchase

It was a difficult period. People didn't know, and it was hard to describe the changes in our lives because they were so private. We lived separately and eventually divorced, but we remain loyal to each other. Now we laugh and call ourselves the odd family. The affection has always been there in spite of the difficulty.

GEORGE: In 1987 the Horizon series was given a solo exhibit at the Minnesota Museum of Art: "Horizon: Small Painting Series, 1980–1987." Sixty-one paintings. Sky, water, shore as I imagined them from the studio.

Two exceptions are winter scenes: *Ice Flow. February* and *Ice Break.* These I did directly from drawings, the cold color remembered and painted later.

I gave Briand a choice of whatever painting he wanted out of the show. He picked *Ice Break.* Predominately white, one of the few winter ones. Sure enough, he had the good sense to pick out a good one that related to his memories of the lake.

Jim Czarniecki introduced the show and Joan Mondale spoke. I gave special thanks to Hazel.

The show had already been exhibited at the Tweed Museum of Art in Duluth. It received many reviews. One included this: "For Morrison—as for Ryder, Melville, and Whitman before him—the sea is a symbol of eternity. But within that vast concept, Morrison finds room for continual change, as if change were the pathway to eternity itself." That was good company to put me in.

I was feeling much stronger as the exhibit opened, helped by Walter's ceremony. My life was coming full circle. As a boy, I had carried water up from the lake for our family to drink. Now I was living much of the time by the lake again.

"We were made to be ashamed of being Indian," I told the art critic from the Minneapolis *Star Tribune.* "In my own way I believe in a lot of the old Indian ideas. . . . I like the idea of prayer to give strength, to make you well; and I believe in the healing power of prayer in the Christian sense, as well as the Indian sense."

The series titles, *Red Rock Variation* or *Lake Superior Landscape,* indicate that the paintings relate to Red Rock, where the studio looks out on the lake. Individual titles often use the idea of spirit forms. All of those shapes and things that come from the images on the canvas can relate to spirits. The shapes might suggest objects in the lake or coming out of the water. Often they're irregular, shaped like an amoeba—organic forms that relate to clouds or puddles.

I try to give imaginative titles, to suggest the poetic and romantic. Some come easily, out of my head, but others I have a hard time finding. Sometimes I have people help me. It works out pretty well, but it takes a while. If I'm really serious and set my mind to it, I can do it alone. I put a dictionary and Roget's thesaurus in front of me, then some little cards with ideas.

Some of the paintings evoke lyrical thoughts, with references from a diverse range—Shakespeare, James Baldwin, Chippewa mythology, even a private reference in memory of Franz Kline. I juggle things around; it's kind of fun.

Ragged Breath: The Rise of Windigo—"broad passages of color as thick as icing," someone said.

Ice Break: Lake Superior, 1985
Acrylic on canvas on board
6¼ x 13¼
Private collection

Downward Wind. Cool Pink.
Red Rock Variation:
Lake Superior Landscape, 1990
Acrylic on canvas on board
6 x 14½
Collection Stephan Hoglund

Ingot Compression—a thick layer of oil on top of acrylic.

Beyond. The Mist—short strokes of paint over alternating cold or warm layers of color, for a pointillist effect.

Alpenglow—rough layers of paint to give a shimmering, bumpy effect.

Spring Interval—light creeping above the horizon, a yellow streak to suggest the moment when you look at the edge of the horizon and see a band of light.

I may put yellow ocher underneath, then lavender scumbled over it. There may be some green in there, too, a complementary color. The artist's prerogative to make the sky lavender.

These were all tricks and methods of applying paint that I have acquired over the years.

As always, I am interested in the phenomena of paint and the act of painting. Using Surrealist ideas and techniques, I let images emerge from the masses of paint. So there may be hidden associations that become real for me in the final mark.

This magic of the artist works with the magic of nature in change. The rock, which I began to regard later in life, has a presence of its own, and the water is a living force, moving and changing. The same with the sky that is constantly changing in the wind—that phenomenon of nature we can't even see, but it has a sound and presence of its own. I've been forming written statements about my art since the early '70s. This is what I wrote for the Horizon series. "I seek the power of the rock, the magic of the water, the religion of the tree, the color of the wind, and the enigma of the horizon."

GEORGE: When I was better and more on my feet from the Castleman's, I had a chance to see a little Australian churinga at the Minneapolis Institute of Arts. About ten inches high, sort of like an ax handle—a dark, flat, oblong stone with some marks on it. It got me curious and I started doing research. The aborigines made many of these stones, or totemic images, to mark gravesites. They vary in size from ten inches to ten feet.

This brought home to me the realization that totems are universal—as small as the little churinga or tall as the sixty-foot poles of the Northwest Coast Indians.

The art institute has put the little churinga away because it's precious, with certain spiritual connections. Louise Lincoln, my friend and curator there, has said that I can see it anytime I want. She realizes that I respect it.

Though many Indians are requesting museums to return sacred tribal objects, I can see the value of a museum taking care of important objects. In the past, sacred objects were in the care of an elder or a shaman; but when a shaman died or religious attitudes changed, or when tribal religions were lost, everything was scattered, wiped out.

Contemporary sculpture, abstract sculpture—like one of Brancusi's beautiful, fluid sculptures—can be spiritual for me as well. But when I began making my own Chiringa Forms, I did them more for their physical beauty. The shape and the tactile quality of the wood appealed to me. I made them oval and wide, not very tall, out of imported woods like purpleheart and padauk, sanded and smoothed. Some have a circle of wood grain in the middle.

I can't make any claims that my Chiringas are spiritual. I do put some magic in the bottom, some herbs and earth, maybe. Maybe that's kosher, I don't know. I did it for fun. There's meaning for me and maybe a few others. I look at it that way.

Chiringa Form, Small #1, 1987
Purpleheart and padauk wood
7 X 5⅜ X 1
Collection Tweed Museum of Art,
University of Minnesota, Duluth
Tweed Associates Purchase Fund

GEORGE: In May 1990 a retrospective of my work, which I had been hoping for when I was so sick, opened at the Minnesota Museum of Art: "Standing in the Northern Lights," titled after one of the Chippewa names Walter Caribou had given me.

The Tweed Museum cosponsored the show; in fact, Steve Klindt, former director of the Tweed, had originated the idea. Then when he left, Katherine Van Tassell at the Minnesota Museum stepped in as curator and was instrumental in borrowing works. She wrote a good essay for the catalog as well.

After its opening at the Minnesota Museum's Landmark Center galleries in St. Paul, the exhibit went to the Tweed in Duluth and, after that, to the Plains Art Museum in Moorhead, Minnesota.

It was a nice thing to see so many of my works together—sixty-seven in all. I hadn't seen some of the paintings for a long time. I arranged for all the loans of work from private collections; I talked to people I hadn't been in touch with for years.

An artist has a connection with patrons that is pretty primary. They own our images!

The range of works in the show was outstanding—four wood collages and, in the catalog, a fine photograph of a fifth, the huge one at the Minneapolis Institute of Arts. Drawings early and later, from *Starfish* and *Dream of Calamity* in 1945, to the big complicated drawings from the early 1970s, to more recent work like *Surrealist Landscape: Leaping Figure* from 1984. That one has two horizon lines—the artist's prerogative.

I liked seeing favorite big paintings from the middle years like *Promenade,* from 1959, loaned by Cape Ann friends Alex and Beverly Roman. I think they owned fourteen of my works, big and small—maybe the largest individual collection before they passed away. They had bought my work when we were young and I was charging very little.

There was a *White Painting* from the Heard Museum, and a good selection from the recent Horizon series, including one of the earliest in that format, *The Badlands,* from 1981, from the Philbrook, where so many years ago my work had been rejected.

The show included a wide selection of totems, too. *Red Totem* from the Heard Museum was reproduced in the catalog, though it didn't make it to the exhibition. The designs on this totem have curves—a nice contrast to the angles and straight lines of the earlier totems.

The show also contained a good sample of my paper collages, works I made off and on from around 1977 to 1984. Some were visual puns on the style of other artists—like *Der Fliegende Hollander: De Kooning Fragment*—where I painted a fragment reminiscent of their style under strips of color suggesting horizon, clouds, sky. In other collages, I discarded the pun and simply chose interesting patterns and textures of paper, even wallpaper, for the bottom segment of these vertical works.

The cover of the catalog was a detail of one of my smaller wood collages. This close-to-the-grain look brought to mind what David Woolley, a curator at the Plains Art Museum, had said: "The first time I saw George's work in the flesh . . . I could not help myself. I had to go up and lay hands on it." He was talking about one of the little Horizon paintings, but the catalog cover had a tactile effect as well.

This was a happy time. I dedicated the retrospective to Hazel and Briand. Friends from my Minneapolis School of Art days came to the opening—Don Davies, who had been in design classes with me, and Audrey Freeman, who like me had majored in fine arts. Seeing them brought back memories of reading the school catalog when I was still at Chippewa City, envious of the so-called big scholarship winners, wishing I could do that.

Museums from all over the country lent works to the show. The retrospective was "a culmination of the total experience of all my exhibiting, and receiving prizes, and being collected by museums" I told Catherine Zaiser of the Fargo and Moorhead *Forum,* in the fall of 1990 when the show went to the Plains Art Museum. "I think it's the dream of every artist to have a big show during his lifetime . . . toward the end of one's artistic career. It becomes an honor."

HAZEL: George and I were living apart by then. We had not been an intimate couple for a long time. But in September 1991 I accompanied him to Providence, where he received an honorary Ph.D. from the Rhode Island School of Design. He could not travel by himself, and I thought it would be nice to go with him. We had had friends together there. I wanted to go.

GEORGE: We stayed with friends, in separate bedrooms. We were already divorced in many ways, I guess, after about five years of separation.

It's difficult to say exactly why two people get divorced. Incompatibility, differences of opinions and likes—these things lead to separation. My illness might have had some bearing on it. We had been fairly compatible when we stayed up at Grand Portage together for a year. Then something had happened in the late '80s. At the time, I wasn't aware that my illness had an effect on us, but I have thought of it since then. It's too bad it had to happen, in a way.

HAZEL: We had talked about not divorcing for a while—divorce is often financially difficult on the woman. But on the way home from Providence, George said he wanted a divorce. We had to work to resolve the financial issues, but now we're friends. More than friends—we're family.

GEORGE: Only in more recent times can I understand the idea that I miss being married to Hazel, or to anyone.

Opposite:
Spectator: Busa Fragment, 1984
Paper collage
11⅝ x 5⅛
Collection Tweed Museum of Art,
University of Minnesota, Duluth
Alice Tweed Tuohy Foundation and
Patrons and Subscribers Purchase Fund

GEORGE: At noon I eat at the elderly program at Grand Portage community center. We are mostly Indians, though a lot of other people join, too.

This spring we had an indoor powwow, a special event for the elders. Each of us got a blanket. I'm sorry it was not a good Hudson's Bay blanket, but it was a nice gesture.

At the powwow there was Indian dancing and drumming. Some dancers came down from the reserve at Thunder Bay. They make the powwow circuit, sometimes at their own expense. Or they might be invited by a tribe and get a fee for participating. The dancers wore various regalia; some had just a ribbon shirt. Maybe a pair of moccasins, maybe a simple band around their head. Others were more ceremonially dressed with feathers and beadwork. At a powwow nowadays, you pretty much see a mixture.

I like to watch the way the feathers move in the dancing. Usually, the tip of the feather is fastened in a cylinder on a band around the dancer's head. The feather is attached with a piece of thong or string so it won't come out. It moves with the movement of the dancer, bobbing his head, bending over and dancing to the rhythm of the music. The dancers imitate animals or birds when they are dancing.

Some dancers still wear jingle dresses. Originally jingles were made of silver, but now some are made of snuff covers. The snuff covers have a steel coating; they're shiny all the time. You take the Copenhagen snuff covers and pound them in such a way as to make a kind of bell. Old jingle dresses are very elaborate, very expensive. I've seen some on Navaho dancers.

I have never been into dancing and singing—I think, primarily because of my leg. One could probably do it anyway, in spite of that, but I didn't. If I were to begin my life over, I would probably get into dancing and singing. I think Indian people should do it. But some people do such things more readily than others. That's the way it goes.

At powwows there are categories of dancing—for elders, for youngers, for children. And some for women. Women are more subdued, they're more modest in their dancing. I don't know why, maybe a cultural thing. When they ask elders to dance, we just walk around in a circle. Walk around a couple of times and that's it. It's our way of being a part of the ceremony, getting everyone to do their part, their prayer.

I still continue with totems. Every totem has a different feel to it. My later totems have included exotic woods—bocote, bubinga, purpleheart and padauk, rosewood, mahogany, wenge, teak. The best example of this kind is in the lobby of La Salle Plaza in downtown Minneapolis. It's twenty-one feet high and two feet square. I cut out different pleasing shapes and stained the lighter woods with color, trying to maintain certain Indian colors—red, blue, yellow, and some green. I deliberately did it that way and employed some animal, bird, weather, and plant imagery—a beaver, for instance, and some leaves, along with a lightning bolt and suggestions of water or clouds. Not realistic, but semiabstract interpretations of these elements. It makes for a very active and colorful totem.

This is about two blocks from my granite mosaic on the Nicollet Mall. I designed the mosaic and the city had it constructed, with fourteen variations of tone from light to dark. I put some Indian suggestions in the 200 pieces, but they are somewhat lost in the abstract design.

La Salle Totem, 1991
Exotic and dyed wood
construction
249 x 24 x 24
La Salle Plaza, Minneapolis

I've traveled to the Southwest a number of times in the last twenty years. The Morning Star Institute was instrumental in helping me meet a lot of artists, showing with them, attending conferences. I've been in Santa Fe once or twice, once to Taos in 1992 for a conference of American Indian writers and artists, including some I had met already—Kay WalkingStick, a Cherokee who lives in New York, and Frank LaPena from California.

Perhaps the most important recent show was "Shared Visions: Native American Painters and Sculptors in the Twentieth Century," curated by Margaret Archuleta and Dr. Rennard Strickland at the Heard Museum in 1991. It showed the Native American Fine Art Movement, as they called it, in the contexts of older traditions of Indian art and Western and world art.

I like the idea of being part of the Native American Fine Art Movement. The term distinguishes Indian fine art from crafts. There were no crafts in the show—no moccasins, no pottery, beadwork, or clothing.

There was a painting in the show by Jaune Quick-To-See Smith, my friend from Montana, titled *Rain*—one of the few abstractions in the show besides my work, *The White Painting,* and Kay WalkingStick's *Uncontrolled Destiny.* They all come from ideas that are not clearly Indian the minute you look at them.

The curators put my painting in a group called "New Indian Painting 1940–Present," along with Oscar Howe, Joe Herrera, and Patrick Des Jarlait, also an Ojibway from Minnesota, from Red Lake. Mine is the only abstract work in that group.

"Morrison was the first and most prominent Indian artist on the New

George at the dedication of his Nicollet Mall mosaic, Minneapolis, 1992.
© 1997, Star Tribune/Minneapolis-St. Paul

York art scene," wrote Archuleta. "He considered himself to be an Indian who is an artist, rather than an Indian artist."

Would I put it that way?

I don't say that I'm any particular kind of artist. I'm an artist who happens to be Indian. I'm not doing strictly Indian themes. I'm an artist pretty much in the mainstream, even though I have been in Indian shows, by virtue of being Indian.

The sculpture section of "Shared Visions" included my *Chiringa Form: Small #1* and a small totem I did for the Northwest Area Foundation. Allan Houser's work was there, too. He's sometimes called the grandfather of contemporary Native American sculpture. Before 1940 there was little Native American sculpture, unlike Indian painting, which has had many generations and styles. We sculptors looked like originators. So there you go again with contemporary Indians doing things in their own way based on modern technology and imagery.

I was included in other Indian shows in the early '90s as well, like "Our Land / Ourselves: American Indian Contemporary Artists," curated by Jaune Quick-To-See Smith at the State University of New York in Albany in 1991. My Horizon painting *Spirit Path. New Day. Red Rock Variation: Lake Superior Landscape* was in the show and created a beautiful cover for the catalog. That was a nice thing.

The catalog essays give a good sense of the history of what Strickland and Archuleta were calling the Native American Fine Art Movement. It seems that Oscar Howe had protested being rejected from the Philbrook's annual in 1958 for much the same reason that my work was not accepted: It didn't fit the criteria for "traditional" Indian art. He had written to the curator to protest: "Are we to be held back forever with one phase of Indian painting that is the most common way? . . . [Will] the Art World . . . [be] one more contributor to holding us in chains[?]"

I wish the Grand Portage council would approach me about getting something of mine for the new community building. Maybe they will. I don't know if people on the reservation understand what I'm doing. We'll have to see . . .

A totem outside would be nice, though the metal work would be expensive. But if I were asked, I could at least find out what the cost would be and make a proposal that they could accept or not.

Not many on the reservation question me about my art. I wish they would recognize the fact that I'm an artist, a local artist who could make something for the community.

They could at least be curious. Indian people are not direct, but if they wanted to know, they could go in a roundabout way to find out.

I have made large outdoor sculptures—not many, but some. For example, I made a five-foot Chiringa for the Fond du Lac Tribal and Community College in Cloquet near the Fond du Lac Reservation. It's done in bronze. The commission came through the Minnesota Percent for Art in Public Places Program. I was one of two artists involved.

A sculptor friend in New York did a lot of the fabricating. For the base we selected a great big boulder that weighs about three to four tons and had it transported to Cloquet. The bronze Chiringa is bolted right into the rock.

I've seen it only once in its setting, where it looks kind of small, lost in the trees. I'd like to see it again. Maybe I'd get a different viewing next time. It varies with the time of day, season, and weather.

I'd also like to see something of mine like that on my own reservation.

One of the elders who eats at the community center with me is Ellen Olson. She speaks the Chippewa language and has become quite well known for her beadwork. She and Ernie, her husband from Grand Marais, went to New York in 1994 for the same reason I did—to attend the opening of the Heye museum. Three people represented Grand Portage, a very obscure Indian settlement in northeastern Minnesota, at this big national Indian museum.

For years the Heye Foundation's museum was in a rough area of Manhattan you sometimes couldn't get a cab to. But now the huge collection of Indian art and artifacts, begun early in the century by a wealthy New York banker named George Gustav Heye, was going to have three sites. The one we were celebrating was a National Historic Landmark building called the Alexander Hamilton U.S. Custom House in lower Manhattan.

The museum opening was attended by over a thousand people. There were a few speeches and a few awards. I didn't get any, but one of my Iroquois friends, Oren Lyons, got an award for outstanding work as an activist—he's a painter, too. We have been to conferences together, and to Cuba.

In the late '80s, the Witch Tree had been threatened. The owner of the land that led down to the tree wanted to sell the land. People from the reservation, including Hazel and me—in fact people from Cook County, from Minnesota as a whole, and maybe even further—came together to form Friends of the Witch Tree. Many had known about the tree when they came up to the North Shore as summer tourists.

We helped create a beautiful poster of the tree, with photographs by Craig Blacklock. Selling the poster and gathering contributions, we raised enough to buy the property.

Then the land was donated to the Grand Portage band. The trail down to the tree was rebuilt with a platform overlooking the tree. Now you can't go right down to the tree anymore. A railing restrains you. That is all to the good.

Then in the middle '90s, there was controversy again about the Witch Tree. We heard that some jerks had chipped off a piece of the bark or wanted to carve their initials in it. Stupid people.

That got things going. The tribe became interested in trying to stop people from going there at all. There was word of trying to halt any picture taking of the tree or even image making.

Hazel came up to try to make her opinions known. She had been using the tree as a primary image in her work. We took a trip to the Witch Tree and

Witch Tree Variation, 1988
Crayon, colored pencil,
and ink on paper
9 x 7
Collection Tweed Museum of Art,
University of Minnesota, Duluth
Alice Tweed Tuohy Foundation Purchase

made an offering of tobacco as we had always done, in the old ceremonial ways. I guess that helped her a lot.

The Indians in Grand Portage stick together as a community. I guess it's an inherent thing about people—they stick together. Not too many Indians even go to Grand Marais to shop. By and large, they stay at the reservation. I think part of it is prejudice.

What is true of us is true of Indians on many reservations. Grand Portage has an enrollment of around 940. Maybe 330 are on the reservation; the rest are living elsewhere—Duluth, Minneapolis. So-called educated Indians leave to get jobs. Those who don't have education may go to the cities, too, and get menial jobs or live on welfare. They may become dissatisfied, return to the reservation, and then may go back and forth until they're deadlocked between two situations.

Since the Indian population in this country is only a fraction of one percent of the total population, they often get lost in general society. That may be why, as in Grand Portage, they remain pretty much to themselves.

We can't go back to living in tepees, of course. But I always encourage retaining some of our Indianness. One of the best places to do that is the Institute of American Indian Arts in Sante Fe. As one of the major art schools in the United States, it draws students from all over the U.S. and Alaska. These days, the school is pretty free-spirited: I think the students are doing what they want to do.

That's the way I'd approach it, if I taught there. I wouldn't twist their arms to do Indian things. But if they wanted to, I would certainly encourage it, by all means. A lot of good Indian artists are coming out of that school.

In 1993 an interview with me came out in the *Akwe:kon Journal* published at Cornell University. Akwe:kon means "all of us" in the Iroquois languages.

The young man who interviewed me was Sam Olbekson, of the White Earth Anishinabe in Minnesota. He was a student in architecture at Cornell. When he asked about the Indian connection in my work, I told him, "I call it pretty much straight painting. If there's any 'Indian' coming through, it's because I am Indian and I'm painting what's coming out of me."

But I do pay attention to Native American artists working today. "I'm very proud to be in shows of Indian artists," I told him. "I guess I'm just one of many working in different ways and I'm glad to be in with that whole group." My advice to the next generation: "Finish school, whether you are going to the Santa Fe Indian School or a university like Cornell."

When I work, I'm not disciplined in the sense of some artists who paint for so many hours, then have lunch, then go back to painting. I'm not like that—I'm more sporadic. I might work intensely for days or weeks at a time. Then I might stop for that length of time and come back again.

I hope the revelations come along the way. One wants continually to make the best possible work.

Seeking the unknown is something I always use. Sitting at the table to work because I've been sick, working in an easy manner, saturating the idea of the Horizon series in small paintings. Now I feel that I am playing them out. I'm doing my last little Horizon paintings. Now I want to go to a larger format, which might change the idea.

Always unfinished. I see art in a broad sense. It's like the composer trying to seek the unknown. Seeking unknown possibilities through sounds.

On the radio recently, I heard a program about people recording sounds in the rain forest. Sounds emitted from the earth, the rustling of the earth. A bird cry in the distance. Water trickling. A musician might incorporate that into his head to interpret nature in his music.

You have to keep going to reach the inevitable point. Whenever that is. Maybe never.

When I had my small apartment near the art institute in Minneapolis, I hung works by many artists I'd traded with. Now some are waiting to be hung here at Red Rock. There are works by Kay WalkingStick—a diptych nicely balanced with an abstraction on one half and a waterfall on the other—and by Frank LaPena—he does ritualistic figures in a landscape.

Fritz Scholder is one of the most well known of the Indian artists—probably the most successful, too. He and R. C. Gorman. But I consider Scholder more original in his work. The print I own, *An Indian Figure*, is a challenging image, with dark background and almost raw surface.

Amy Cordova's figures all have that round face, a common image for her figures. But they don't have a commercial look; every one stands on its own. They seem to come right out of her in a nice way.

Frank Bigbear I find playful, because he does things like powwows with crazy configurations within the image, and a conglomeration of colors. The Bockley Gallery in downtown Minneapolis handled his work, and mine, too, before it went out of business.

Frank and I have also been in shows together. He was a student of mine for a while and may have gotten some ideas from me. He's been successful in getting grants. I applied for some of the same ones but never got one.

The art we have around us has a strong effect. I believe in that. Around my bed at Grand Portage, the art is all by friends. You could say I have a wall of abstraction and a wall of Native American work. I didn't arrange it this way; it just happened.

On the abstract wall are works mostly by artist friends and colleagues that I traded with in my New York days. Pearl Hardaway, Hyde Solomon, Albert Kresch, Hugh Mesibov, Virginia Banks, Sol Bloom. There's also a batik by my first wife, Ada.

I have a piece by Herman Somberg, a New York artist who came to teach at the University of Minnesota. There's also one by Minneapolis artist Virginia Bueide, who helped us find the church; and one by my art school chum, Maria Stueland; then a recent work by a new friend, Pam Davis, now in New Mexico.

On the Native American wall, above my pillow, is an eagle feather from Walter Caribou, one of the two he gave me at the healing ceremony. This one hangs above me as I sit in bed and look out at the lake. The other, hanging from the rearview mirror in my car, is wearing out from blowing so much.

I also have a raven feather, my animal totem, hung above the bed for good luck. There's a choker, too, of bone and ermine tails, made by a young Native American artist. I wear it on occasion.

On my other walls, beside the big sliding glass doors out to the deck, hang other works. Some are mine—my old painting of two fish and the "Mystery Still Life" that I consider a masterpiece from long ago.

Above the old jeweler's table, I have two big prints: one by Jaune Quick-To-See Smith and one by Hazel, *Woods' Floor: Path to the Witch Tree.* In 1983 Hazel and I each made prints to sell and raise money for Saint Paul Academy. This was her print; mine was *Red Cube,* an image of red, interlocking curved shapes.

On the shelves is my collection of glass. I've been interested in glass as a medium for years, and I've known glassblowers and made swaps. At one time I had collected 150 colored glass goblets and 150 plain ones. I like them arranged on open shelves. They catch the light and the colors glow—gold, red, deep blue.

They say that singing and chanting and dancing are now very important in many tribes throughout the United States. These traditions, with their own kind of ceremonial structure, help to carry on the tribal religion.

I have tobacco with me all the time, even in the car. I sometimes burn it at parties or meals. We used to do it at Thanksgiving meals or a New Year's dinner.

Hazel always had a New Year's prosperity dinner, which came from her Dutch background. At the dinner I introduced tobacco as part of the ceremony. Also sage—that's common with the Southwest Indians. Sage is part of their ceremonial offering to the spirits. The Chippewas burn it; I do, too. They say when you burn tobacco and sage, the smoke carries the message to the spirit.

Here in Grand Portage I have the peace pipe made by Bob Rose Bear. It's a nice large pipe, with a bowl shaped almost like a cross. There's an eagle inlaid in silver into the pipestone. The long stem is a certain kind of wood, maybe ash, and is decorated with beads and muskrat fur around the neck.

It is a prized possession of mine. I have used it in certain kinds of make-believe ceremonies. Like the prosperity dinners. We would burn some sage or tobacco and then I'd smoke this pipe and pass it around. This make-believe thing is kind of a carry-over from what I've seen and heard. I wouldn't want to prove that I know about all those ceremonies. I just follow them in my own way.

Lately I've added to my magic. Ernie Whiteman, an Indian artist from the Twin Cities, gave me some tobacco. And Tom Morin, a colleague from the

George and his "wall of abstraction," ca. 1990.
Courtesy of George Morrison

Rhode Island School of Design, sent me some rice, maybe from Mexico, that he thought was very special. So I added that.

It's an ongoing mixture, though I've slowed up in the last year or two. The basic things are there. I think all the ingredients have a healing power. And it smells wonderful.

I also often think of the feather in one way or another. I think of the Indian dancers with the feathers in their hair, turning as they move. I see the image of the feather turning. Then I think of the fact that birds can fly in any kind of weather. When they're wet, they shake their feathers and replenish the oil from a gland. I keep the two feathers from Walter Caribou nearby. I have also had both of the names from Walter written on my business card.

My immune system has been affected by the Castleman's and the radiation and chemotherapy treatment. Now I have sores on my hands and feet. They take a long time to heal, but they do seem better, after almost a year.

I can't expect to live forever. I hope Hazel and Briand will put a stone for me in the Morrison section of the Chippewa cemetery. It's across the highway from the Chippewa Church, the one my grandfather helped found. My ashes can be spread on the lake, but I'll have a marker, too. Having it both ways.

I saw the seasons coming this year. Here on the lake, it's so temperate, and it's so rich. I've seen it many times before, but sometimes you think about it with another twist.

Every moment, the horizon is present. The horizon has been an obsession with me for most of my life. It makes an indelible image that, for me, stems from being born and growing up near the edge of the lake. Later, spending many summers on the Atlantic shores reinforced it.

I think of the horizon line as the edge of the world, the dividing line between water and sky, color and texture. It brings up the literal idea of space in a painting.

From the horizon, you go beyond the edge of the world to the sky and, beyond that, to the unknown. I always imagine, in a certain surrealist way, that I am there. I like to imagine it is real.

Notes

INTRODUCTION

2 Morrison's Native American heritage: Following Morrison's practice, this introduction uses the terms Indian, Native, and Native American interchangeably; the same with Chippewa, Ojibway, and Anishinabe. Morrison also calls his hometown Chippewa City and Chippewa Village interchangeably; the text of his story will use Chippewa City to avoid confusion.

4 "Native American Fine Art Movement": Archuleta and Strickland, "The Way People Were Meant to Live," in *Shared Visions* (1991), p. 5, 9.

5 "broke the ice": Rubin, "Arshile Gorky," in *New York Painting and Sculpture,* by Geldzahler, p. 375.

5 At the same time: Chrysler later brought his collection to what is now the Chrysler Museum of Art in Norfolk, Virginia.

6 Fifty years before: Raff, *Pioneers in the Wilderness,* p. 69, 155, 156.

9 I had written about him twice: Galt, "A Rage for Order," in *Artpaper* (1986), and "Art from Red Rock," in *Mpls. St. Paul* (1989).

SKY LAYER: ATTENTIVE WATERS

21 Rendezvous Days: This annual event commemorates the fur trade tradition at Grand Portage when, at the end of the season, the traders and voyageurs would gather to be paid and to dance, drink, eat, and swap stories.

21 The 100th anniversary of the church: Father Urban Steiner, O.S.B., served the Catholic churches, including St. Francis Xavier, in Cook County, Minnesota, from 1979 to 1985. See "Benedictines Leave North Shore," June 27, 1985, and "Fourth of July Celebration at St. Francis Xavier Church," July 4, 1985—both in *Cook County News-Herald* (Grand Marais, Minn.), p. 4.

23 Mary Caribou, my grandmother: See "Mrs. James Morrison of Chippewa City is Dead," *Cook County News-Herald,* Dec. 18, 1924, p. 4, which gives her first name as Marie.

23 I remember my grandfather Morrison: See "Coroner's Report" and "James Morrison, Sr., Dies"—both in *Cook County News-Herald,* May 5, 1927, p. 1.

23 My great-grandfather was born: These dates are approximations, part of family history. George's sister Mary Morrison Dahmen remembers that their grandfather died in his late seventies. That would put his birth around the 1847 date that George remembers.

24   My mother was born: Fort William, Barbaba's birthplace, is in Ontario, Canada. Her family later moved to Cook County.

24   When she was seventeen or eighteen: See "Topics of a Week," *Cook County News-Herald,* Nov. 25, 1915, p. 1.

25   Indians in this area lived anywhere: According to the Treaty of La Pointe, signed in 1854 by the Chippewa of Lake Superior and the United States, each Chippewa head of a family or single person more than twenty-one years of age might be assigned eighty acres of land. In 1856 the federal government surveyed a village plot at Grand Portage and gave a lot of approximately one-half acre to each Indian who would build a house on it. Chippewa City was not located on reservation land. See U.S., *Indian Affairs: Laws and Treaties,* compiled and edited by Charles J. Kappler (5 vols.; [Washington, D.C.]: GPO, 1975), vol. 2:649; Alan R. Woolworth and Nancy L. Woolworth, "Grand Portage National Monument: An Historical Overview and an Inventory of Its Cultural Resources," 1982, vol. 1:190, typescript in Minnesota Historical Society Collections (hereafter MHS).

26   I was born at home: Morrison was born on September 30, 1919. See "News-ettes of Grand Marais and Vicinity," *Cook County News-Herald* (1919), which describes him as a "daughter."

31   Then the Depression came: The federal Works Progress Administration, part of President Franklin Delano Roosevelt's plan to combat the Great Depression, put many people to work. WPA workers conducted oral-history projects, painted murals in public buildings, and upgraded city services, such as building the sewer in Grand Marais. The WPA program was not welfare.

35   My father died; His brother Joe died: See "James Morrison Dies at Cloquet," Dec. 1, 1949, and "Joe Morrison Dies at 64," Feb. 9, 1950—both in *Cook County News-Herald,* p. 1.

37   Hayward, Wisconsin, Indian school: The Hayward Indian School was run by the U.S. Office of Indian Affairs (later the Bureau of Indian Affairs) in northwestern Wisconsin. See Eldon Marple, *The Visitor Who Came to Stay:*

Legacy of the Hayward Area (Hayward, Wis.: Country Print Shop, 1971), p. 83–84.

39   That's when they sent me: A sanatorium for Indians with tuberculosis was operated at Onigum, Cass County, by the Office of Indian Affairs from 1924 until it burned in January 1935. See J. Arthur Myers, *Invited and Conquered: Historical Sketch of Tuberculosis in Minnesota* ([St. Paul?: Minnesota Public Health Association], 1949), p. 485–486.

39   My older brother: The state-run Minnesota Sanatorium for Consumptives, located across Leech Lake from Onigum, was popularly called Ah-Gwah-Ching, which means "outside" in Ojibway. A separate building for Indian patients, constructed and operated with federal funds, opened there in August 1935. See Annual Reports, 1934–1935, 1935–1936, Ah-Gwah-Ching Sanatorium (Minnesota State Sanatorium) Records, Minnesota State Archives, MHS.

MEETING BEFORE THE HARD DISTANCE: PATHWAYS

43   The high school principal: Elizabeth Maryhart was both the principal and an English teacher at Grand Marais High School from 1935 to 1938. See "School Opening Postponed One Week," August 29, 1935, p. 1, and "The School," January 12, 1939, p. 2, 3—both in *Cook County News-Herald.*

46   When I was seventeen: The Civilian Conservation Corps (CCC), which included an Indian Division, was one of President Roosevelt's favorite and most successful work programs. During the Depression, it provided young men with employment in conservation projects such as reforestation, rural improvement, and forest-fire protection.

47   the Minneapolis School of Art: The school was renamed the Minneapolis College of Art and Design in 1970.

EXTENDED PATH: VIOLET WATER

65   That summer I showed a portrait: George's painting, *Old Woman,* received an award in the "Portrait" category. See 1944 catalog in collection of Minnesota State Fair Annual Fine Arts Exhibition catalogs, MHS.

75   This second gallery: Clipping in Morrison scrapbook from undated brochure for Grand Central Art Galleries, New York.

81   The year of my one-man show: The titles of Morrison's paintings sometimes changed over time. *Starfish* is also known as *Starfish and Whalebone* and may be the work identified as *Shell and Starfish* in the brochure for his 1948 show at Grand Central Moderns.

85 One reviewer noted: Unidentified clipping in scrapbook.

DREAMS OF DESTINATION: EARTH SONGS

97   I met Jackson Pollock: The Cedar Street Tavern, 24 University Place, was a favorite bar for artists and such Beat Generation writers as Allen Ginsberg, Jack Kerouac, and Gregory Corso.

CONVERGING OF THE GREEN: FIRE RIDGE

137   Artists tend to mold their environment: Nelson, "Artists Create Home in Former Church," *St. Paul Pioneer Press* (1972).

138   After they were released from prison: See Weyler, *Blood of the Land.*

141   In 1972 the Walker Art Center: The exhibition, "American Indian Art: Form and Tradition," was organized jointly by the Walker Art Center, the Minneapolis Institute of Arts, and the Indian Art Association, a regional group.

141   As an art critic wrote: Steele, "The Past: Art with a Purpose," *Minneapolis Tribune* (1972), p. 4.

141   The newspaper also published interviews: Anderson, "The Present: Is There `Indian' Art?," *Minneapolis Tribune* (1972), p. 18, 20.

146   Patricia Hobot . . . said: Quoted in Martin, "Art Collection of Infinite Horizon Fits Morrison Well," *Star Tribune* (1987).

150   The allotment act: The federal General Allotment Act (Dawes Act) of 1887 authorized the allotment of tribal land to individual Indians and the sale of remaining land.

151   Minneapolis American Indian Center: The original name was the Minneapolis Regional Native American Center. It was designed by Thomas H. Hodne Jr. of the Hodne-Stageberg Partners.

155   When Evan Maurer wrote: Maurer, *Native American Heritage* (1977), p. 131.

160   Earlier definitions of Indian art: In the early 1980s Indian artists themselves began writing about the definition of Indian art. George C. Longfish encouraged the "lifting of these constraints which romanticized Indian life to a stylized and repetitive simplicity." He pointed out that the issue of authenticity—whether you were "Indian" enough—was not the artist's problem. See Longfish and Joan Randall, "Contradictions in Indian Territory," in *Contemporary Native American Art* (1983), p. [13].

CEREMONY INTO THE LIGHT: ORACLE

166   She described our studios: Hart, "Of Horizon and Spirit," *Lake Superior Magazine* (1986), p. 34.

167   "[Walter] spoke of the responsibility": Belvo, "Introduction," in manuscript for proposed book about Horizon paintings.

172   One included this: Riddle, "George Morrison," in *New Art Examiner* (1988), p. [67].

173   "broad passages of color": Riddle, "George Morrison" (1988), p. [67].

175   This is what I wrote: Morrison, "Artist's Statement," in manuscript for proposed book about Horizon paintings.

175   I began making my own Chiringa Forms: Morri-

son uses the spelling "chiringa" for his small sculptures. Some museums have corrected the spelling to "churinga" on the works they acquired.

178 This close-to-the-grain look: *Standing in the Northern Lights,* videocassette produced by Kuusisto and Gumnit (1991).

182 "Morrison was the first": Archuleta, "Catalogue Raisonné," in *Shared Visions* (1991), p. 91.

183 "Are we to be held back": Hill, "The Rise of Neo-Native Expression," in *Our Land / Ourselves* (1991), p. 2.

184 the opening of the Heye museum: For a description of the museum and its exhibits, see Bruchac, "The Heye Center Opens in Manhattan," in *Smithsonian,* p. 40–49.

192 These last statements are drawn from Morrison, "Artist's Statement," in manuscript for proposed book about Horizon paintings, and Erickson, "An Interview with George Morrison," in *Artpaper* (1987), p. 28.

SELECTED BIBLIOGRAPHY

MANUSCRIPTS

Belvo, Hazel, ed. Manuscript for proposed, untitled book about Horizon paintings by George Morrison. Includes "Introduction," by Belvo; "George Morrison: An Appreciation," by Jamake Highwater; and "Artist's Statement," by Morrison. Ca. 1987. In possession of Belvo.

Morrison, George. Scrapbook. Ca. 1944–1961. In possession of Morrison.

ARTICLES, EXHIBITION CATALOGS, BROCHURES, PRESS RELEASES, REVIEWS, AND VIDEORECORDINGS

1919

"News-ettes of Grand Marais and Vicinity." *Cook County News-Herald* (Grand Marais, Minn.), Oct. 8, p. 1.

1944

"George Morrison Wins Art Award at State Fair." *Cook County News-Herald*, Aug. 31, p. 1.

1946

John K. Sherman. "Surrealist Ranks Swell at Woman's Club Salon." *Minneapolis Star-Journal*, Apr. 9, p. 12.

"Morrison, Goldstein, Sonoda." Brochure in Morrison scrapbook (hereafter "scrapbook") for exhibition at Ashby Gallery, New York City, Mar. 16–Apr. 16.

"George Morrison Featured in Three-Way Art Exhibit." *Cook County News-Herald*, Mar. 21, p. 1.

"Art Student Plans New York Exhibit." *Duluth News-Tribune*, June 30, Cosmopolitan section, p. 6.

"Critics' Show." Brochure in scrapbook for exhibition at Grand Central Art Galleries, New York City, Dec. 10–21.

Edward Alden Jewell. "Ex-GI's Art Wins Critics' Show Prize." *New York Times*, Dec. 11, Late City ed., p. 28.

Jo Gibbs. "New York Critics Nominate New Talent." *Art Digest* (New York), Dec. 15, p. 12.

Ca. 1946

"The Eye and the Lens." Flyer in scrapbook for exhibition at Pyramid Gallery, New York City, Sept. 20–Oct. 2.

1947

Catalog of the Twenty-seventh Annual Exhibition. Catalog in scrapbook for exhibition by Rockport Art Association, Rockport, Mass., June 28–July 29 (first part), and Aug. 2–Sept. 7 (second part).

Lawrence Dame. "Regarding Art." Clipping in scrapbook from *Boston Herald,* apparently July 6.

Howard Devree. "Matters of Moment at Midsummer." *New York Times,* July 27, Late City ed., section 2, p. 8.

First Biennial Exhibition of Paintings and Prints. Clippings in scrapbook from catalog for exhibition at Walker Art Center, Minneapolis, Aug. 21–Sept. 28.

1948

"George Morrison: Paintings." Brochure in scrapbook for exhibition at Grand Central Moderns, New York City, Apr. 27– May 8.

Helen Carlson. "Diversified Solo Exhibitions." Clipping in scrapbook from *New York Sun,* Apr. 30.

Carola Kaufmann. "Kunstchronik." Clipping from *National-Zeitung* (Basel, Switzer.), June 15, Evening ed. "Art Chronicle." Typescript of undated translation by unidentified translator. Both in scrapbook.

1949

Earl Finberg. "Ex-Duluthian to Exhibit His Art at Gallery Here." *Duluth Herald,* Apr. 25, Final Home ed., p. 18.

_____. "Morrison's Art Sincere, Notable." *Duluth Herald,* May 2, Final Home ed., p. 20.

_____. "East U.S. Mecca for Artists." *Duluth News-Tribune,* Dec. 11, Women's Activities section, p. 2.

1950

P[esella] L[evy]. "Morrison's Quarry Colors." *Art Digest,* May 1, p. 3.

"George Morrison: Gouaches—Oils—Drawings." Brochure in scrapbook for exhibition at Grand Central Moderns, May 2–13.

1951

"Third Tokyo Independent Art Exhibition; Troisième exposition des artistes indépendants de Tokio." Flyer for exhibition in Tokyo, with related postcard. Both in scrapbook.

1952

"New York: Members Summer Exhibition 1952." Brochure in scrapbook for exhibition at Grand Central Moderns, May 26–Sept. 30.

A[line] B[.] L[ouchheim]. "By Groups and Singly." *New York Times,* June 1, Late City ed., section 2, p. 7.

"George Morrison Wins Paris Scholarship." *Cook County News-Herald,* July 17, p. 1.

"Two Local Artists Exhibit Far Away." *Duluth News-Tribune,* July 20, Women's Activities section, p. 8.

1953

C.-H. Sibert. "Directions d'un jeune art américain." Clipping from *Arts spectacles,* Jan. 9–15, Paris ed. "Directions of Young American Art." Typescript of undated partial translation by unidentified translator. Both in scrapbook.

Peintres américains en France. Catalog in scrapbook for exhibition at Galerie Craven, Paris, Apr. 24–May 7.

G. M. "Peintres américains de Paris à la Galerie Craven." Clipping from *Combat: Le journal de Paris,* May 4. "American Painters in Paris (Craven Gallery)." Typescript of undated partial translation by unidentified translator. Both in scrapbook.

Louis-Paul Favre. "Grand Central Moderne de New-York." Clipping apparently from *Les arts* (Paris), July, with typescript of untitled, undated partial translation by unidentified translator. Both in scrapbook.

_____. "Les peintres américains." Clipping from *Combat: Le journal de Paris,* July 13. "Article in Combat, July 13th, 1953." Typescript of undated partial translation by unidentified translator. Both in scrapbook.

1954

Earl Finberg. "Career Artist." *Duluth News-Tribune,* Feb. 28, Cosmopolitan Feature section, p. 5; see also photograph of Morrison, p. [1].

Stuart Preston. "Diverse in Aims." *New York Times,* Mar. 14, Late City ed., section 2, p. 10.

Finberg. "Morrison Exhibit Hung in Tweed." *Duluth News-Tribune,* Nov. 7, Women's Activities section, p. 8.

"Contemporary American Indian Painting." Brochure in scrapbook for exhibition at M. H. de Young Memorial Museum, San Francisco, Nov. 25, 1954–Jan. 2, 1955.

Alfred Frankenstein. "Survey of Indian Art at de Young Museum." *San Francisco Chronicle,* Dec. 1, Final ed., p. 23.

1955

"Invitation to Opening." Brochure in scrapbook for Federation of Modern Painters and Sculptors, Inc., annual exhibition at Riverside Museum, New York City, Nov. 13–Dec. 4.

1956

Senta Bier. "Twenty-nine Works Are Shown in Whitney Exhibit at Speed." Clipping in scrapbook from *Courier-Journal* (Louisville, Ky.), Dec. 9.

1957

"George Morrison: Paintings" and "George Morrison: Paintings[,] January 25–February 13, 1957." Brochure and press release in scrapbook for exhibition at Grand Central Moderns.

"'Whitney Annual' Exhibit Opens Today." Clipping in scrapbook from *Quincy* (Ill.) *Herald-Whig,* apparently Feb. 10.

"James Gallery Invitational Annual." Flyer in scrapbook for exhibition at James Gallery, New York City, May 16–June 15.

1958

"George Morrison: Recent Paintings: April 15–May 3, 1958." Press release in scrapbook for exhibition at Grand Central Moderns.

"George Morrison Honored at Impressive Reception." *Cook County News-Herald,* May 8, p. 1.

1959

"Kilbride to Show Work of Indian Artist Morrison." *Minneapolis Tribune,* Feb. 1, Editorial-Business section, p. 7.

"Paintings by George Morrison Opening Friday, February 6th." *The Potboiler* (Kilbride-Bradley Art Gallery, Minneapolis), vol. 6, no. 1, Feb., p. 1. Copy in scrapbook.

John K. Sherman. "George Morrison's Art Lyrical and Subjective." *Minneapolis Star,* Feb. 13, p. 8A.

"Spring Invitation." Flyer in scrapbook for exhibition at Nonagon gallery, New York City, May 12–June 4.

"Phoenix Invitational 1959." Flyer in scrapbook for exhibition at Phoenix Gallery, New York City, May 15–30.

"More Art Than Money." *Vogue* (New York), Dec., p. 118–121.

1960

Betty A. Dietz. "New Yorker, Here to Teach, Sees Art Changing Rapidly." Clipping in scrapbook from *Dayton* (Ohio) *Daily News,* Feb. 7.

1965

"George Morrison . . . is here on vacation." In "Shore Lines" column, *Cook County News-Herald,* July 29, p. 8.

1968

T. H. Littlefield. "Rhode Island Designers Exhibit Work at Skidmore." Photocopy of undated clipping from unidentified source. In possession of Morrison.

1969

"Artist Honored." *Minneapolis Tribune,* May 10, p. 19.

1972

Carole Nelson. "Artists Create Home in Former Church." *St. Paul Pioneer Press,* Mar. 5, Final City ed., Family Life section, p. 1, 6.

American Indian Art: Form and Tradition. Catalog for exhibition organized by Walker Art Center, Indian Art Association, and Minneapolis Institute of Arts, at the Walker and the IDS Center, Minneapolis, Oct. 22–Dec. 31.

Mike Steele. "The Past: Art with a Purpose," p. 4–5, 7–13.

Brian Anderson. "The Present: Is There 'Indian' Art?,"

p. 18–24, 28–29. Both in *Minneapolis Tribune,* Oct. 22, Picture section.

1973

George Morrison: Drawings. Catalog for exhibition at Walker Art Center, Apr. 15–May 27. Includes "George Morrison and Philip Larson: An Interview: St. Paul, 28 February 1973," by Larson, p. [3]–[7].

Mike Steele. "George Morrison Weaves Heritage into Landscapes." *Minneapolis Tribune,* Apr. 22, p. 6D.

1976

Mike Steele. "Native American Son Brings Artistry Back Home." *Minneapolis Tribune,* Dec. 19, p. 1D, 12D.

1977

Evan M. Maurer. *The Native American Heritage: A Survey of North American Indian Art.* Catalog for exhibition at Art Institute of Chicago, July 16–Oct. 30.

1980

Judy Vick. "Vision of Art vs. Reality of Marriage." *Twin Cities* (Edina, Minn.), Oct., p. 76–81, 136–138.

1981

Confluences of Tradition and Change / 24 American Indian Artists. Catalog for exhibition organized by Richard L. Nelson Gallery and C. N. Gorman Museum, University of California, Davis, in cooperation with Museum of the Southwest, Midland, Tex., at the university, Jan. 19–Feb. 27, and the museum, Apr. 25–June 7. Includes "Confluences," by Allan M. Gordon, p. 4–7.

1982

Eight Native Minnesota Artists. Catalog for exhibition at Minneapolis Institute of Arts, June 4–July 25.

Thomas O'Sullivan. "Artists Portray North Shore's Witch Tree." *Minnesota Volunteer* (Minnesota Department of Natural Resources), July–Aug., p. 48–51.

1983

Douglas Ross. "George Morrison; Stuart Nielsen." *New Art Examiner* (Chicago), Jan., p. 21.

Ann Baker. "Artist Couple Are Far from Matched Set." *St. Paul Pioneer Press,* Mar. 4, Minnesota ed., p. 1B.

George Morrison: Entries in an Artist's Journal. Catalog for exhibition at University Gallery, University of Minnesota, Minneapolis, Mar. 28–May 1. Includes title essay by Lyndel King, p. 4–5.

Judith Raunig-Graham. "George Morrison." *Report* (University of Minnesota publication for faculty and staff), June, p. 7.

Contemporary Native American Art. Catalog for exhibition at Gardiner Art Gallery, Oklahoma State University, Stillwater, Oct. 1–28. Includes "Contradictions in Indian Territory," by George C. Longfish and Joan Randall, p. [11]–[15].

1984

Adelheid Fischer. "George Morrison." *Arts* (Minneapolis Society of Fine Arts), Feb., p. 22–23.

1986

Margot [Fortunato] Galt. "A Rage for Order: The Long Lives of Ten Minnesota Artists." *Artpaper* (Visual Arts Information Service, Minneapolis), vol. 6, no. 1, Sept., p. 17–19.

John Camp. "Artist Confronts Life, Death." *St. Paul Pioneer Press and Dispatch,* Sept. 7, Metro Final ed., p. 1A, 11A.

"The Artist and His Work." *St. Paul Pioneer Press and Dispatch,* Sept. 7, Metro Final ed., p. 10A.

Joanne Hart. "Of Horizon and Spirit: Grand Portage's Most Famous Artists Draw from Nature's Palette." *Lake Superior Magazine* (Duluth), Nov.–Dec., p. 32–37.

1987

Elizabeth Erickson. "An Interview with George Morrison." *Artpaper,* vol. 6, no. 30, summer, p. 28.

Traditions and Innovations: Seven American Artists. Catalog for exhibition at Plains Art Museum, Moorhead, Minn., Oct. 1–Nov. 29.

Mary Abbe Martin. "Art Collection of Infinite Horizon Fits Morrison Well." *Star Tribune* (Minneapolis), Nov. 15, Minneapolis ed., p. 1G, 3G. Article about "Horizon: Small Painting Series 1980–1987," exhibition at Minnesota Museum of Art, St. Paul, Nov. 14, 1987–Jan. 17, 1988.

Jim Billings. "George Morrison's Universe." *Vinyl Arts* (St. Paul Art Collective, Minneapolis), vol. 4, no. 8, Dec. 3, p. 14.

1988

Mason Riddle. "George Morrison." *New Art Examiner,* Feb., p. [67].

"Ojibwe Art Expo Winners." *The Pioneer* (Bemidji, Minn.), Apr. 19, p. 5.

Minnesota Artists Look Back: 1948–1988. Catalog for exhibition at Minnesota Museum of Art, Oct. 16–Dec. 31.

1989

Margot [Fortunato] Galt. "Art from Red Rock." *Mpls. St. Paul,* Mar., p. 58, 60–61.

1990

Standing in the Northern Lights: George Morrison, A Retrospective. Catalog for exhibition organized by Minnesota Museum of Art and Tweed Museum of Art, Duluth, at Minnesota Museum, May 6–June 24, and Tweed Museum, July 28–Sept. 9. Includes "Standing in the Northern Lights," by Katherine Van Tassell, p. 18–33.

Mason Riddle. "Exhibit Captures Aurora of Minnesota's Morrison." *Star Tribune,* May 10, Minneapolis ed., p. 1E, 10E.

_____. "George Morrison." *Arts Magazine* (New York), Oct., p. 105.

Catherine Zaiser. "Minnesota Artist Displays Works in Tune with Nature." *The Forum* (Fargo, N.Dak., and Moorhead, Minn.), Oct. 11, p. A10.

1991

Standing in the Northern Lights. Videocassette produced by Linda Kuusisto and Daniel Gumnit; directed, written, and edited by Kuusisto. 30 min. Gracie Productions.

Our Land / Ourselves: American Indian Contemporary Artists. Catalog for exhibition at University Art Gallery, University at Albany, State University of New York, Feb. 1–Mar. 17. Includes "Essay," by Paul Brach, p. 5–6; "The Rise of Neo-Native Expression," by Rick Hill, p. [1]–4; and "The Color of the Wind," by Lucy R. Lippard, p. 7–15.

Shared Visions: Native American Painters and Sculptors in the Twentieth Century. Catalog edited by Margaret Archuleta and Rennard Strickland for exhibition at Heard Museum, Phoenix, Ariz., Apr. 13–July 28. Includes "The Way People Were Meant to Live: The Shared Visions of Twentieth Century Native American Painters and Sculptors," by the editors, p. 5–11; and "Catalogue Raisonné," by Archuleta, p. 71–101.

"Artist Creates Huge Totem for Plaza." *Cook County News-Herald,* July 22, p. 9.

Dan Hauser. "Nouveau Totem." *Skyway News* (Minneapolis and St. Paul), Aug. 20–26, p. 20.

1992

Chris Waddington. "Art Elevates the Skyways." *Star Tribune,* Feb. 18, Minneapolis ed., p. 1E.

Jeffrey Kastner. "Environmental Essence: His Work Reflects Morrison's Link to Nature." *Star Tribune,* Mar. 12, Community Zone 7 ed., Variety section, p. 6E.

"Mosaic on the Mall." *Star Tribune,* June 11, Minneapolis ed., p. 1B.

We, the Human Beings: Twenty-seven Contemporary Native American Artists. Catalog for exhibition at College of Wooster Art Museum, Wooster, Ohio, Aug. 26–Oct. 19. Rev. 2d printing, 1993.

1993

Sam Olbekson. "Beyond the Horizon: An Interview with Anishinabe Artist George Morrison." *Akwe:kon Journal—All of Us Journal* (American Indian Program, Cornell University), vol. 10, no. 1, spring, p. 26–34.

Chuck Haga. "Fledgling Painters Brush Shoulders with Acclaimed American Indian Artist." *Star Tribune,* June 24, Minneapolis ed., p. 1B, 5B.

BOOKS

"George Morrison, Ojibway / Chippewa Painter and Sculptor." In *This Song Remembers: Self-Portraits of Native Americans in the Arts,* ed. Jane B. Katz, p. 53–60. Boston: Houghton Mifflin Company, 1980.

Highwater, Jamake. "George Morrison." In *The Sweet Grass Lives On: Fifty Contemporary North American Indian Artists,* p. 148–152. New York: Lippincott & Crowell, 1980.

Kostich, Dragoš D. *George Morrison.* Minneapolis: Dillon Press, 1976.

Wade, Edwin L., ed. *The Arts of the North American Indian: Native Traditions in Evolution.* New York: Hudson Hills Press in association with Philbrook Art Center, Tulsa, Okla., 1986.

_____, and Rennard Strickland. *Magic Images: Contemporary Native American Art.* Tulsa, Okla.: Philbrook Art Center; Norman: University of Oklahoma Press, 1981. Based on "Native American Arts '81" exhibition at the Center, Aug. 2–Sept. 6, 1981.

Wyckoff, Lydia L., ed. *Visions and Voices: Native American Painting from the Philbrook Museum of Art.* Tulsa, Okla.: The Museum, 1996.

GENERAL REFERENCES

Arnason, H. H. *History of Modern Art: Painting, Sculpture, Architecture, Photography.* 3d ed. New York: Harry N. Abrams, 1986.

Bruchac, Joseph. "The Heye Center Opens in Manhattan with Three Exhibitions of Native Arts." *Smithsonian,* Oct. 1994, p. 40–49.

Raff, Willis H. *Pioneers in the Wilderness: Minnesota's Cook County, Grand Marais and the Gunflint in the Nineteenth Century.* 3d ed. Grand Marais, Minn.: Cook County Historical Society, 1988.

Rubin, William. "Arshile Gorky, Surrealism, and the New American Painting." In *New York Painting and Sculpture: 1940–1970,* by Henry Geldzahler, p. 372–402. New York: E. P. Dutton, 1969.

Rushing, W. Jackson. *Native American Art and the New York Avant-Garde: A History of Cultural Primitivism.* American Studies Series. Austin: University of Texas Press, 1995.

Weyler, Rex. *Blood of the Land: The Government and Corporate War against the American Indian Movement.* New York: Everest House Publishers, 1982.

INDEX OF ARTWORKS ILLUSTRATED

Alternate titles (in parentheses) follow main titles.

PHOTO CREDITS